Praise

"How can you build the successful sales practice you have dreamed of having? Nick Ray in his marvelous new book, "There's More to Selling Than Making the Sale", leads us through not only the sales process, but all the steps needed to build a well-designed and prosperous sales business. During his incredibly successful career in the financial services industry, he has chronicled all the systems and processes he has used and now shares those secrets as a blueprint for easy management and stunning success."

Ginger Cockerham
Master Certified Coach and
author of *Magnificent Masters in Financial Services*

"Sales plateaued? Frustrated? Have a high desire to double or triple your sales volume in the next 12 - 24 months? Nick Ray, a top industry producer, gives you over 30 years of his wisdom, practical tools and techniques on how to build a prosperous financial services business. This book is filled with straight talk – no fluff or filler. Nick will make you a winner!"

Jim Horan
President
The One Page Business Plan Company

"Nick Ray's book on selling really hits the mark. Follow his road map and you won't get lost on your way to making more money – a lot more money."

Katherine Vessenes, JD, CFP(R), RFC and
author of *Building Your Multimillion Dollar Practice*

"A successful salesperson is not necessarily a successful business person. This book will help you become both. You'll learn how to avoid the sales rollercoaster and build a practice you'll be able to sell when it comes time to retire."

Charles Legalos, PhD
President, Critical Contacts, Inc.

There's More to Selling Than Making the Sale

There's More to Selling Than Making the Sale

A step-by-step approach
to increasing sales
and building a prosperous
financial services business

Nick Ray
CLU, RHU, ChFC, MBC
Business Coach

SALES SOLUTIONS PRESS
Berkeley, CA

SALES SOLUTIONS PRESS
16000 Ventura Boulevard
Suite 1103
Encino, California 91436

Visit our website at www.SalesSolutionsPress.com

Publisher's Cataloging-in-Publication Data

Ray, Nick
Building a Center of Influence Engine:
"The Relationship System" / by Nick Ray.
Includes appendices.

ISBN 978-0-984-2900-0-0 (PB)
1. Selling. 2. Financial Services. 3. Success in Business. 4. Title.
658.85
HF5438.25 .R39 2010

Set in Berkeley Oldstyle and Frutiger
Book Design by Lori Gudmundson
of Creative Vision Arts, Inc.
Printed in U.S.A.

About the Author

NICK RAY is a 40-year veteran of the financial services industry who has transformed his stellar sales career into a prosperous coaching practice serving financial services professionals. He is a 30 years + Life Member of the Million Dollar Round Table and is a Lifetime Member of the Leading Producers Round Table. He is a Chartered Life Underwriter, Registered Health Underwriter and a Chartered Financial Consultant, as well as being designated a Master Business Coach.

In addition to this full-length book for sales professionals, Nick has written several sales workbooks and columns for numerous financial services publications. He is a popular speaker on building successful sales careers. Nick lives in Berkeley, California, with his wife Ellen and his dog Jake. Nick and Ellen have seven grandchildren who keep Nick – and Jake – on their toes.

This book is dedicated to all those
Financial Service professionals and entrepreneurs
who are courageous enough
to truly serve their customers and clients
and to lead a meaningful life.

Table of Contents

Introduction

The genesis of this book began more than forty years ago, when I was a newly recruited Northwestern Mutual Life agent. My early career began on a promising note: I sold about 50 policies in my first nine months in the business, and then hit the wall when I ran out of prospects to call on. Little did I know that what I didn't know then would, one day, be the basis for this book.

I left personal production several years ago as I began the transition from insurance and benefit sales to business coaching for financial service professionals and entrepreneurs. What initially surprised me was the dramatic lack of essential and basic sales and business training available to these professionals. I thought they would be given excellent training in these areas:

- Job / industry fit
- Marketing channel selection
- Opening a case procedures
- Fact finding systems
- Buying committee guidelines
- Closing a case
- Sales coaching and motivation
- Keeping helpful sales records
- Developing and implementing a useful business plan
- Administrative support procedures and systems guidance
- Career evaluation guidelines

I found the training for all these issues to be spotty at best. I set out nearly a decade ago, when I began my coaching practice, to discover the best tools with which to help my clients. I have gained valuable information and training from coaching more than 300 individual clients and having attended hundreds of sales conferences, sales seminars, and agency sales / client builder meetings. It is the culmination of these efforts, and over 40 years of personal sales and business experience, that are brought together in this book. Inside these pages you will discover effective and useful ideas addressing these key issues.

My purpose in the writing of this book is to provide guidelines for dealing with issues from the beginning to the end of a financial services career. From the selection process, to the sales process, to the administrative processes and finally to exit time when you retire or sell your practice, you'll find guidance to help you on your way. The final chapter provides you with a chance to engage in a comprehensive evaluation of your practice. As advisors, our goal is not just to earn a paycheck, but to be people who serve others and lead a life filled with meaning and integrity. When you take a look at how you're doing – and where you've been – I hope you like what you see.

That is why this book is titled *There's More to Selling than Making the Sale.* This book is truly about how to live well, while building and maintaining a successful financial services career.

I hope you'll use this book as a primer on how to integrate all these diverse elements into an effective practice and a meaningful life.

ONE

Are You a Good Fit?

The best example of the American dream is to be in business for yourself. The chance to make something that's yours, and the chance to control your own time and your own destiny is very high in the pantheon of American values. That's why entrepreneurs and people involved in financial services find the sales business so attractive: in addition to helping people achieve financial security, they can also be their own boss!

The problem comes when reality doesn't match one's expectations. The most dramatic example of how difficult it is to make a sales career a good fit is to examine statistics in the financial services industry. In a conversation with Howard Stevens, CEO and chairman of consulting and assessment firm HR Chally Inc., I learned that faulty agent selection processes may result in failure rates of as much as 80-90% by the end of the 4th year, for the least qualified candidates. Put another way, it means that if you and seven of your new associates were in the same sales training class, at the end of the fourth year only one of you would still be in a sales position. To some extent this is to be expected because the barrier to entry into sales is often low. Thus, good people who are not suited for a sales career often leave the business when they discover a sales career is not a good fit. That fact alone does not explain why the agent retention rate is so low. Other reasons, listed below, provide an explanation for this dismal and painful result.

Personal interview, 10/14/09.

The purpose of this chapter is to give you tools to improve the odds. What if, instead of only one out of eight surviving in the field, one out of four survived? Not only would this double the recruiting and training success rate; it would also offer a huge emotional and financial savings for all parties involved. In later chapters we will examine the complete sales process, in order to further improve your odds of becoming a successful financial services professional.

There are three basic steps that can dramatically improve the odds of increasing agent retention, whether you're a recruiter or a candidate looking for a sales position. Following these three basic steps will help both of you determine whether a sales career is a good choice, and make sure that a thoughtful training program is in place to help ensure continued success.

The Three Steps to Sales Success

1. Ensure that the candidate meets *eligibility* guidelines.
2. Ensure that the candidate meets *suitability* guidelines.
3. Make sure that each candidate hired completes an initial *sales training program* and participates in the ongoing 3-Legged Sales Training Program.

In this chapter we will look more closely at the "the three steps to sales success" from the candidate's perspective; in the following chapter we will look at these three steps from the employer's perspective.

Step 1: Eligibility

Determining the eligibility of a candidate is a process of *discovery* rather than *persuasion*. Candidates should not simply try to sell themselves to a potential employer. An attitude of discovery is key; you should always know the basic requirements needed to be a good candidate for the position you seek before you actively pursue any sales positions. The basic problem with either side using persuasion as the first tool is that the manager/recruiter or a candidate can often convince the other party that there is a good fit. Very persuasive people can often make poor hiring decisions. This usually occurs when eligibility standards are unclear or absent.

The Candidate Eligibility Assessment Process

Did you investigate the potential employer prior to the job interview?

Do you have an up-to-date resume?

Can you verify each claim made on your resume?

Can you describe your strengths and weaknesses for each aspect of the sales cycle?

See "The Sales Process" chart on page 64.

Can you describe your target market?

See the *Invisible Market Matrix* at SalesSolutionsPress.com.

What more do you need to discover about the job you are considering?

What is your objective when being interviewed for a sales position?

Determine If You Are Eligible

Are you, the candidate, actually eligible for the position? The fact that a recruiter or manager would hire you only means that you are eligible from *their* point of view; what truly matters is that the position meets *your* eligibility requirements.

The person hiring you can't do the work involved to make the sale – you will. That means that you, as the candidate, have to know what kind of sales position you're looking for.

You should have very well-defined guidelines for each of the three steps to success (eligibility, suitability, training). For example: Assume that you're looking to enter the financial services industry and a major financial services company has openings. Ask yourself: "What are the skills I should have in order for this career to be a good fit?"

Show You Are Eligible

As a candidate for a sales position, you need to be able to provide a detailed explanation for each of the accomplishments stated in your resume. If you said that you had obtained X number of new clients in the past year, you should be able to tell your prospective employer how you acquired those new clients. If you say you have an excellent sales closing ratio, you should be able to tell the prospective employer what that closing ratio is – and why it's excellent. If you've developed a new territory, you should be able to tell the prospective employer how you developed the territory and what your sales accomplishments were.

Discover the Requirements for the Position You Seek

If you are a candidate for a financial services position, it is imperative that you discover the eligibility requirements for any sales position you are seeking. Then you will have benchmarks (just as the employer does) to help you discover if this – or any sales position – is right for you.

How do you discover the eligibility requirements before the interview? The thoughtful and thorough candidate will do research on the prospective employer via the internet – Google, for example – and will learn as much as possible about the company. Next, you should talk to other employees about the company and get as much information as possible about the company's prospects and its direction. Also, talk to other salespeople (if you can) to get a feeling about the sales opportunity being offered.

Armed with this information, you are now in a position to ask the interviewer: "My research indicates that the job has basic eligibility standards (state what you've learned). Are there other eligibility requirements that you have in addition to the ones I just mentioned?"

The answer should be revealing. If the interviewer says there are no other requirements, you've done your homework well. Or, you may discover the interviewer doesn't have specific eligibility requirements – in which case, you'll have to decide if this position is a good one to pursue.

The interviewing process described above may be much more structured than what you have actually encountered. Research has indicated that structured interviews are much more accurate in selecting viable candidates. You, as the candidate, will have to evaluate the sales interviewing process as to its accuracy in presenting the actual job requirements. A well-structured interview indicates that the employer has given serious thought to eligibility requirements, which is a good indicator that you are getting an accurate picture of the position itself and its requirements.

What happens if you get the job – but it's not the position you thought it was? Unhappiness, disappointment, wasted time, and more can result. Perhaps you've relocated and now find yourself in a bad job – and in a strange city as well. None of these consequences are desirable. So take the extra time and effort to do your research to ensure a more positive outcome to your job search.

Green, *Get Talent!*, 74-76.

A Healthy Attitude

A genuine interest in determining if there is a good fit for the position you seek will be appreciated by the potential employer. Do your homework and come prepared with good questions about the make-up of the firm and if, and where, you see yourself fitting in.

Fluffing up a resume and trying to make yourself look better often works against a candidate in the long run. Boldly asserting your chief assets is encouraged, but not if you overstate the truth. You may talk yourself into a job for which you are not qualified. Throughout the interviewing process, honesty, integrity and accountability are fundamental prerequisites to ensure that a good hiring decision is made. A good decision can only be made if you are clear about the eligibility requirements and discover that you meet these requirements.

At the end of the eligibility phase of the interview, the prospective candidate should feel satisfied that the basic job requirements have been fully described and discussed. You can then ask yourself: is this a position I wish to pursue?

Key Eligibility Guidelines for Candidates

- ❖ Make sure you are aware of and are prepared to answer basic eligibility questions.
- ❖ Be clear and honest about your skills and experience.
- ❖ Be able to verify all your resume highlights.
- ❖ Be truly interested in discovering if the job is a good fit for you.
- ❖ Google and research your potential employer to obtain as much background information as possible.
- ❖ During the job interview, ask about the prospective employer's industry position, financial position and sales training program.
- ❖ Do not try to make the job fit. If it's right for you, it should be a natural fit.
- ❖ Be willing to say no to a job offer if it's not a win/win situation.

Step 2: Suitability

Only when the candidate has met the eligibility standards can we move to Step 2 of the hiring process: 'suitability'. The fact that someone is eligible for further consideration does not mean that the candidate is automatically suitable for the position.

As a reminder, *eligibility* requirements are based on measurable, observable and verifiable facts. *Suitability* for a position is based much more on who you are – the internal attitudes, beliefs, values and interests that govern your behavior. It is these values and attitudes that will ultimately determine your success as a financial services professional.

Assessment Tests as a Suitability Tool

The Gallup organization, in its book *First Break All The Rules,* discovered that our personality and style are pretty much hardwired by the time we become teenagers. It is imperative that we acknowledge and recognize that who we are – is who we are. While we usually continue to change as we mature, my experience is that our basic strengths and personality characteristics are essentially unchangeable.

Buckingham and Coffman, 81.

Assessment instruments are important tools to help discover true motivation and desires. Suitability is not specifically about personality. Rather, it is finding people who have the same level of desire, who have the same willingness to work and persevere, and who have the same competitive spirit, who have the same interest in dealing with objections and overcoming hardships that characterize all competent salespeople.

If you, as the candidate, discover that you don't meet the suitability skills that are fundamental for the sales position, then this position is not a good fit for you. Your own self interest should encourage you to stop the hiring process at this point.

The Candidate Suitability Assessment Process

Have you discovered your sales strengths and weaknesses?

How did you do this?

What are your character strengths and weaknesses?

Do you know what kind of sales training program you need?

Do you have a well-defined target market?

What are your income expectations from a sales position?

In 1 year:

In 3 years:

In 5 years:

Assess Your Suitability

If you're the job candidate, you can take assessment tests and discover your strengths and weaknesses. Remember: everybody has strengths and weaknesses. The Profile XT and Harrison Assessment are two examples of excellent assessment tools that I use with my clients.

Trying to fit yourself into a job that suits you poorly won't work. Even if you get the job, you will probably pay a high price in the long run. The purpose of this book is to help you discover the things you're best suited for, in an efficient fashion, but not to persuade you to try to be somebody you're not. Too often, people recruiting oversell the job, and people looking for a job oversell their skills.

A battery of assessments is available through Nick Ray. See "Assessments" at coachnickray.com.

Key Suitability Guidelines for the Candidate

- ❖ Discover your own strengths and weaknesses by using, for example, The Chally Assessment, Profile XT, TTI Sales Strategy Index and the Harrison Assessment. These assessment instruments can also reveal areas where coaching can be very helpful in improving your sales skills.
- ❖ Ask your potential employer about the company's sales training program.
- ❖ Talk with other salespeople and ask to sit in on a sales training class.
- ❖ Develop your target market profile and compare it to the target market of the company you are considering.
- ❖ Obtain a clear picture of sales targets, bonuses and the total sales compensation package.
- ❖ Be willing to say "no" if the job is not a good fit.

See *Target Market* workbook at coachnickray.com for more information about target marketing.

Know Who You Are

When looking for a sales position, or trying to obtain a sales position, candidates often think "I can make it happen," or, "I can change to meet the job requirements." But as stated earlier, we know that people fundamentally don't change, nor should we expect them to. Similarly, companies have well-defined cultures and personalities, and we should not expect the company to change in order to meet the requirements of an individual candidate.

That's why it's critically important that a candidate knows what an ideal situation is, and a company has clear guidelines about what type of candidate best suits their needs.

I recommend two books that are helpful in the eligibility and suitability processes:

1. For the recruiter / employer:
   Get Talent! By Paul C. Green, PhD, Skilfast Inc, 2007.
2. For the candidate:
   Get Hired! By Paul C. Green, PhD, Skilfast Inc, 2006.

Step 3: Sales Training

My experience indicates that salespeople fail for two basic reasons:

1. The candidate was not a good fit for the job. (They did not meet eligibility and / or suitability guidelines.)
2. Even if they were a good fit, the lack of an effective initial training program and an ongoing sales training program results in a greatly diminished chance of success.

A 3-Legged Sales Training Program

The best sales training program has three legs (discussed in detail in Chapter Two):

1. Leg number one is regular *observation*.
2. Leg number two is regular and thoughtful *feedback*.
3. Leg number three is *motivation* to help the sales representative stay on track.

In my long career in sales, no supervisor ever observed me during a selling call. This may strike you as being strange, but in fact it's probably typical. The most effective sales operations exist where the sales manager is really a sales *coach*.

In the interview process, ask important questions regarding the employer's sales training program and your supervisor's approach to overseeing the work you do. If you are aware of your need for training and regular sales coaching, and discover that you will be working independently in an outlying office with only the occasional phone support, then the job prospect may not be a good fit for you. Look for that helpful coach – you'll be happy that you did. Getting regular sales training is nourishing to the soul and helpful for your checking account. Success as a financial services professional is very dependent on having a supportive sales training program. Again, remember that a good assessment tool will reveal your sales skills needing training or improvement.

Are You A Good Fit?

A successful career in sales is challenging and demanding and should be entered into with courage and care. Making sure the position is a good fit for you will ensure that your decision will have a positive professional outcome.

TWO

Is This Candidate a Good Fit?

When evaluating a candidate, it is important to use a model which measures all the important characteristics necessary for the position. What follows is an example of a basic business plan for an agency seeking to grow.

Every business plan has 5 basic steps. Here is an example of an agency business plan:

1. A clear *vision* of what you'll accomplish in a specific tim frame: E.g. "We'll generate $X in revenue in the next twelve months."
2. A clear definition of your *mission*: Why you are doing what you're doing. "We'll build a successful financial services agency though careful candidate selection and consistent sales training."
3. Clearly defined *objectives*: "We'll hire and begin training six new associates in the next twelve-month period."
4. Sound *strategies*: "We'll define our eligibility and suitability guidelines, use proven assessment tools, and implement a proven sales training program."
5. Specific *action plans*: "We will select a recruiting consultant within the next 90 days. We will investigate assessment tools by the start of our next sales quarter." Action plans: what by when.

Your candidate selection processes should include all 5 steps listed above; see my example below. In my experience, the typical business plan for the candidate selection process is largely non-existent, or at the very least full of holes. Otherwise, we would not hear statements such as:

- "Let's throw it up against the wall and see if it sticks." (Or perhaps "see if the candidate sticks.")
- "You just can't find good people anymore."
- "Agents won't fill out fact finders like they should and then they don't make the sales they should."
- "They spend too much time on coffee breaks and not enough time on the phone."

The problem with all these statements is simple: They reflect a lack of clarity about how to hire and how to provide effective sales training.

How do you obtain that clarity? By developing a One Page Business Plan that addresses the steps you should take to select a good candidate. The following example gives you an idea about how you might structure your plan.

See "The One Page Business Plan" at coachnickray.com.

A Sample Candidate Selection Business Plan

Following is an example of a business plan for selecting good candidates and building an agency:

VISION: Our agency will generate $1 million of revenue in the next 12 months.

MISSION: To create a highly successful agency that is built on respect for the client, the company, and the advisor.

OBJECTIVES:

- Recruit six new advisors in the next 12 months.
- Develop eligibility and suitability guidelines within 90 days.
- Select a new sales training program within 180 days.
- Institute a sales coaching program within 180 days.

STRATEGY: We will meet our training objectives by hiring a consultant(s) to design and help us implement our selection and training programs.

ACTION PLANS:

- Set up a recruiting program with our agents and outside recruiters by __/__/__.
- Search for consultants who can help us design structured interviewing programs by __/__/__.
- Search for consultants to help us select and use assessment tools.
- Look for sales training program consultant to help us select a new sales training program by __/__/__.
- Roll out interviewing program by __/__/__.
- Roll out new sales training program by __/__/__.

On the Road to Improvement

As mentioned earlier, when only about 1 out of 8 candidates succeed (industry average), there is obviously significant room for improvement. This chapter will offer three basic ideas about improving your selection and training programs. These are the same issues discussed in Chapter One; this chapter is focused on the people doing the hiring, rather than those being hired.

The Three Steps to Sales Success:

1 Ensure that the candidate meets *eligibility* guidelines.

2 Ensure that the candidate meets *suitability* guidelines.

3 Make sure that each candidate hired completes an initial *sales training program* and participates in the ongoing 3-Legged Sales Training Program.

Each of these important components will start with an assessment of how well you think your current hiring and training practices are working.

Step 1 – Eligibility

Determining the eligibility of a candidate should be a process of *discovery* rather than one of *persuasion*. A sales manager/employer/recruiter should avoid the temptation of trying to persuade a candidate to join their company. What's important is to have a keen understanding of the requirements for the position, and then engage in a thorough process to determine if the job eligibility requirements have been met. An open-minded attitude of discovery is the key to good candidate selection.

The basic problem with using persuasion as the first tool in the candidate selection process is that a persuasive manager / recruiter can often convince the candidate that there is a good job fit. Talking about the incredible potential for this job (which may only happen rarely) usually leads to disappointment on the part of the candidate if that potential doesn't materialize. Very persuasive people can often make poor hiring decisions. This usually occurs when eligibility standards are unclear or absent. The fundamental goal is to generate long-term agent retention, not simply to achieve shorter-term hiring goals.

What you should be trying to discover: Is the candidate a good fit for the job? If the fit is good, then no undue persuasiveness is required. The goal is to have clearly defined eligibility standards that can be used in the hiring process.

The Employer Eligibility Assessment Process

Do you have specific eligibility guidelines?

Did you evaluate your key salespeople to generate these standards?

Have you tested the validity of your eligibility guidelines?

Are your eligibility guidelines predictive of success?

Do you have social and cultural guidelines as part of your eligibility standards?

Do you have a standardized eligibility interview process?

Do you check references?

What are you looking for in a resume?

Do you have a well-defined target market?

Do you evaluate the candidate's target market with regard to your target market objectives?

See the *Invisible Market Matrix* at SalesSolutionsPress.com.

What Are Eligibility Requirements?

An important – and useful – mindset is to operate using Steven Covey's Habit #2: Begin with the end in mind. In effect, we need to reverse-engineer the sales position and ask:

Covey, 95-194.

- What are the appropriate eligibility requirements for this position?

This simple question opens up a number of important issues. For example:

- Do you have eligibility requirements for your operation? If so, what are they?
- Have you done any research on these eligibility requirements? Have you tested your assumptions – or do you merely have an opinion? Do your eligibility requirements predict future success?
- Is there consistency across your organization when determining candidate eligibility guidelines?

The essential issue is that your eligibility standards should be based on the inherent requirements of the actual job itself. It is often suggested that these standards can be determined simply by evaluating your best salespeople and deriving a composite of their skills.

This is a method that will not withstand scrutiny, because any good salesperson will have a combination of positive and negative characteristics.

The question becomes one of discernment. It's not simply a composite you are looking for, but rather a list of eligibility standards that are predictive of future success. I'm sure you can think of many salespeople whom you would not want to clone – regardless of their sales success. It is often surprising how unpleasant top salespeople can be. Using this example, we should ask: What skills and background would the perfect candidate possess? He / she might have:

- 3 years of sales success – *if* – that sales success could be verified
- They might have been a competitive athlete – *if* – you have verified proof athletic experience predicted future success
- They might be a college graduate – *if* – you could prove that being a college graduate was a causal factor for success
- They might be impeccably dressed – *if* – being well-dressed was predictive of sales success

The point, then, is to establish standards that have a predictive cause and effect relationship with sales success.

How do you discover what you're looking for? Assemble a group of 3 to 5 people – sales manager, recruiter, office manager and successful salespeople – and ask them: "What are the observable characteristics we should look for when interviewing candidates for our agency?" Some issues you might discover:

- Has a good resume with experience we deem to be important
- Is presentable, but not necessarily perfect
- Has an appropriate level of education and experience
- Is well-spoken and sincere

Every eligibility characteristic you select should meet this simple but critical standard: the characteristic has a provable connection to sales success.

The eligibility checklist produced should be predictive of future sales success. By seeing the characteristics our key people possessed, even before they interviewed for the job, we can generate this list – which is made of observable traits and experience. Using a sports analogy, let's assume you are a college basketball coach, recruiting players for your team. You might come up with this list for the center position:

- Minimum height of 6'9"
- Minimum 3 years high school basketball experience
- Good physical condition: candidate passed the physical exam
- 3.0 GPA or greater
- Averaged at least 10 points and 8 rebounds per game

These are all observable traits, and are minimum requirements for your team. This is a simple yes/no test. Does the player have these traits: "Yes" – continue the interview; "No" – say thank you and keep looking.

Determine If the Candidate Is Eligible

The basic objective of the eligibility interview is to discover verifiable information about the candidate. For a sales position you could ask:

1. "Do you have sales experience? Have you been successful? Please give me an example of a successful sale."
2. When computer applications or technical skills are required, the candidate should understand and be able to demonstrate the necessary skills. In today's leaner sales environment, the computer has often replaced human support. It's typical that a sales position will have little or no human assistance – it's all up to the salesperson himself. Therefore, a candidate may need to have mastery of these basic computer skills:

    - Basic word processing skills, including sending attachments
    - Use of Excel or an equivalent spreadsheet program
    - Use of wi-fi and remote computing skills
    - Ability to create PowerPoint presentations
    - Ability to complete reports – most likely including a CRM (customer relationship management) system

- Use of a smart phone, such as an iPhone, Blackberry, Palm Pilot, etc. This assumes that your phone is part of your regular business activity and has the ability to do remote computing (where available).

You should amend this list to meet your specific requirements.

Decipher the Resume

Another important issue is knowing how to decipher the resume. Obviously, it's very important to either obtain or receive verification of important items mentioned in a candidate's resume.

References should be checked. This step is often overlooked because it can be awkward or time consuming; yet spending the time often yields valuable information. Time spent checking references could prevent you from hiring the wrong person. Today, a former employer is likely to say little about a former employee rather than be negative, for legal and personal reasons. Read between the lines and ask important character questions, such as, "Would you work with this person again? Can you share a time when the candidate went above and beyond the expected? Is he or she a team player? Did this person routinely accomplish stated goals?"

The person doing the hiring should review the resume to evaluate the candidate's skills and accomplishments. If you are hiring, you should ask the candidate when, and how, they accomplished the tasks mentioned in the resume.

Next, the candidate might be asked to demonstrate basic presentation skills. Making a brief imaginary sales presentation could be a very helpful, and useful, requirement to gauge the candidate's presence of mind and presentation skills. If defined sales achievements are mentioned, those accomplishments should be verified. Only those people who meet the job's eligibility standards should be eligible for the suitability section of the interview process.

Eligibility Interview Pitfalls

A mistake that prospective employers often make is to evaluate the quality of the candidate on what are often non-verifiable or non-relevant issues. For example, do you like the way the candidate dresses? Do you like the candidate's personality? Do you like the candidate's school? Do you think that prior employment is a solid indicator of future success? Do you think that asking the popular question, "What is your biggest weakness?" is a good indicator of future success? What is the correlation between a high GPA and success? Are any of the questions you ask predictive of future success?

Every question you ask in the eligibility section of the interview should be relevant to the position being filled. That means that you must know the specific job eligibility requirements in advance of the interview itself. When you have a clear understanding of the relevant job requirements, your questions become more focused, and candidate answers become very revealing and clarifying.

For the Employer: Key Eligibility Guidelines

- ❖ Evaluate your best sales representatives' backgrounds and experience to discover traits that are predictive of future success.
- ❖ Examine your best salespeople's work habits to discover their success patterns.
- ❖ Discover social and cultural patterns required to work with your company's target market.
- ❖ Determine if the candidate has a good connection to your target market.
- ❖ Determine if the candidate's resume is oriented towards describing true talents and accomplishments, or if the resume merely emphasizes making the candidate look good.
- ❖ Develop a sales eligibility profile based on your key salespeople's patterns.

- Develop a standardized interview process using the eligibility profile. (It is recommended that you develop a standardized printed interview form.)

Green, *Get Talent!*, 27.

- Be willing to say "no" to the candidate if it's not a good fit.

Step 2 – Suitability

Employer Suitability Assessment Process

Have you tested your key salespeople to determine their best sales skills and attitudes?

Do you have written suitability guidelines?

Do you have a target market definition?

How do you evaluate the candidate's target market in relation to your company's target market?

Do you get feedback from other key salespeople regarding the candidate's suitability?

Do you give assessment test(s) to measure the candidate's fitness for the job?

On a scale of 1-6, how effective are the tests you are using?

Set Standards

The best way to improve the candidate / job selection process is to create well-defined eligibility and suitability profiles. Suitability standards are often non-existent or poorly defined by employers. That is why Stevens of HR Chally, assessment experts, has said that up to 55% of all salespeople hired are ill-suited for the sales position being offered. Failure to have well-defined suitability guidelines is a sure sign that the selection process is flawed and that agent retention will be lower than desired.

Personal interview, 10/14/09.

As a sales manager or employer, you ultimately need to know the kind of salesperson you're looking for, as your company or agency's success depends on selecting the right candidate. Generally speaking, using only observable personality characteristics is an incomplete method for selecting the right candidate. In my opinion, the most important factor for achieving sales success is an unquenchable desire to succeed. Yet it is often difficult to determine if this attitude is present simply by talking to a candidate. That is why I believe it's so important to have the candidate complete assessment test(s) that will reveal inner (and often unknown) values and attitudes.

Key Sales Success Characteristics

Paul C. Green, PhD, in his book *Get Talent!,* suggests testing for these basic competencies that all successful salespeople have:

- Practical problem solving abilities
- The ability to deal with uncertainty
- Productive coping skills
- Effective goal setting skills
- Individual learning and organization skills
- Strong task orientation
- Demonstrated willingness to serve others
- Good oral communication skills

Green, *Get Talent!,* 74-76.

According to Dr. Green, you should test for 4 to 6 of these competencies in order to evaluate a candidate's chance for doing the job well.

According to The Harrison Assessment, an assessment tool I use, these are the key traits they suggest are predictive of future sales success:

- Wants a challenge
- Takes initiative
- Has good influencing skills
- Has good interpersonal skills
- Has high level of self-acceptance
- Has adequate finance and business skills

Both the interview and the assessment test(s) used should evaluate the candidate's strengths in the critical issues described. The result of using these tests (see information below) is better candidate selection and a more accurate description of those skill or attitude areas needing training or coaching. A candidate need not be perfect, but good agent retention requires good basic skills and a training program where sales coaching can help the salesperson achieve a high degree of success.

Determine Suitability Requirements

The best way to determine appropriate suitability requirements is to evaluate your most competent salespeople and discover the essential skills and attitudes they possess. These evaluations should yield a composite that describes your ideal candidate traits. You can then use this composite skill set to develop useful suitability requirements for your sales position.

Another essential tool for developing suitability guidelines is sales assessment tests. These tests can help uncover and reveal the important personality characteristics that your top salespeople possess. Among the tests we recommend are: Profile XT, The Harrison Assessment, Sales Strategy Index, and The Chally Assessment. These assessments, coupled with your key salespeople traits, will help you develop a composite success profile to help you hire salespeople who possess the inner drive necessary for job success in your sales organization.

Not All Suitability Profiles Are Alike

It's important to keep in mind that not all sales suitability profiles are alike. If the position is in a new territory where little supervision is offered, it's reasonable to assume that you'd need a very self-motivated salesperson. Compare this to a very well-established company with well-established customer relationships and well-defined territories. This position may require much more customer maintenance than customer development. While both of these examples are sales positions, each of these sales positions has considerably different requirements.

If you are the person involved in representative selection, you should use assessment tests that measure the traits needed for your specific job needs. The Chally Assessment process, for example, has identified 14 different sales profiles."

hrchallygroup.com

A Further Refinement of Your Sales Selection Process

It is helpful to categorize your sales candidates to ensure maximum sales effectiveness. We know that a sales representative can fall into one of these four categories:

1. High Skills / High Fit
2. High Skills / Low Fit
3. Low Skills / High Fit
4. Low Skills / Low Fit

How do you use this sales rating system?

CATEGORY 1: HIGH SKILLS / HIGH FIT

A Category 1 salesperson should be hired and nurtured. The company should do for this sales representative whatever is required and is reasonable; this category's representatives are the company's most productive.

For example, if I were a sales manager and had a category 1 salesperson who didn't like paperwork, I would provide him with an assistant. Why? Because the output from this salesperson may be 20, 30, or 40 times the cost of an assistant. In a meritocracy, category one salespeople

– who are high skill and high fit – qualify for the best offices and the most support for a very simple reason: they produce the most profit.

CATEGORY 2: HIGH SKILLS / LOW FIT

This person should be hired only if extensive training is available or if there are other suitable positions within your company. They should not be hired, or retained if already an employee, if training or alternate positions are not available. This is not a marriage made in Heaven.

CATEGORY 3: LOW SKILLS / HIGH FIT

This person should be put in a relatively low risk position, but should be retained and given intensive training if you have training systems already in place. Intensive training may help develop this person's inherent capability to produce good results.

CATEGORY 4: LOW SKILLS / LOW FIT

This candidate is not a good fit for your company, should not be hired, and should be released if already employed by you. No job offer should be made to a category 4 candidate.

For the Employer: Key Suitability Hiring Guidelines

- ❖ Have key salespeople take reliable sales-related assessment tests.
- ❖ Use these assessment test results to develop a suitability profile.
- ❖ Develop and use a standardized suitability interview process.
- ❖ Develop a target market profile for your company using the *Invisible Market Matrix*.
- ❖ Compare the candidate's target market profile with your company's target market to see if there is a good fit.
- ❖ Have the candidate talk with other key salespeople to see if the candidate fits your company's guidelines.
- ❖ Be willing to say "no" if the candidate is not a good fit.

Available at SalesSolutionsPress.com.

Hiring Decision Flow Chart

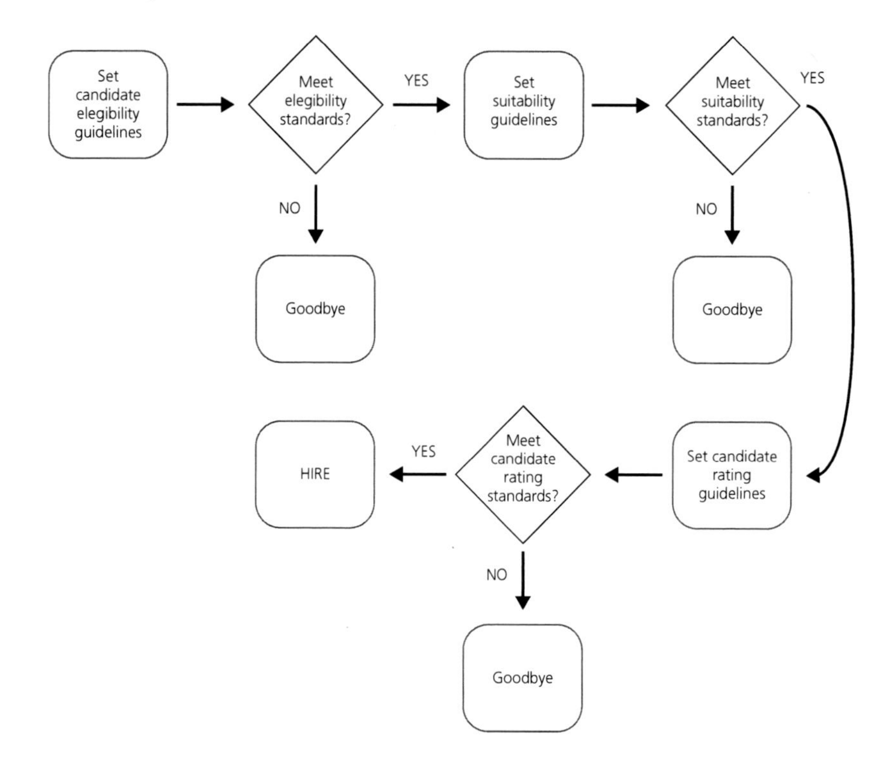

Step 3: Sales Training

We know that salespeople fail for two basic reasons (this section was briefly touched upon in Chapter One):

1. They were not a good fit for the job. (They did not meet eligibility and suitability guidelines.)
2. Even if they were a good fit, the lack of an effective training program resulted in a greatly diminished chance of success.

A 3-Legged Sales Training Program

The best sales training program has three legs:

1. Leg number one is regular *observation*.
2. Leg number two is regular and thoughtful *feedback*.
3. Leg number three is *motivation* to keep the sales representative on track.

In my long career in sales, no supervisor ever observed me during a selling call. This may strike you as being strange, but in fact it's probably typical. The most effective sales operations exist where the sales manager is really a sales coach, or where a sales coach / trainer is available. Let's follow this process with both a sports and business executive.

LEG #1: OBSERVATION – A SPORTS MODEL

Imagine, for example, that you were an effective and successful basketball coach. You would attend every practice. You'd provide feedback, as needed, to every player. You would observe how the players functioned as a team. You would be sensitive to the various personalities on the team. And you'd be interested in keeping the team motivated to maintain a winning attitude.

Salespeople need this support and training as well. As a sales manager or trainer, you should be aware that advisors achieve the maximum level of success when observed on a regular basis. Not just once a quarter, or once every year, but on an ongoing basis until both the observer and the observed feel that a satisfactory level of competence has been achieved.

I don't know of any successful team where the coach does not observe the team members on a regular, continuous basis. Even superstars need coaching – no one can be a superstar without regular observation, feedback and positive motivation. Tiger Woods, the world's best golfer, has a coach. The reason is simple: he can't see his own swing.

Salespeople can't observe themselves in action either. In this regard, they are no different than Tiger Woods. Long term success comes more easily and quickly if we are regularly observed. Whether it's sports or business, the reality of our competitive environment requires regular observation so that we stay focused and receive useful feedback that will, in turn, lead to improved performances.

LEG #1: OBSERVATION – A BUSINESS MODEL

For example, our salesperson, Carol, is about to experience her first observation. Her manager/coach might say something like: "Carol, I'm just going to be a fly on the wall. Just relax and go through your regular presentation. We'll talk after the interview."

LEG #2: FEEDBACK – A BUSINESS MODEL

Feedback is next. The best feedback is the type that concentrates on only the important issues: the ones that are most germane and relevant to creating and sustaining success. Effective and useful feedback, if provided in a neutral and caring way, will help the salesperson improve performance. Feedback helps the salesperson improve because it offers specific and usable recommendations.

On the other hand, feedback given in a negative fashion is often injurious and will not necessarily be helpful. Studies I've seen suggest that it may take at least five positive affirmations to offset one negative or negatively inspired comment. Think about how you feel when you are involved in an argument with a boss, partner, spouse or friend. Negative and hurtful comments are often hard to get over. The coaching position is one where the purpose of feedback is to help the person improve – not embarrass or criticize them, which is ultimately counter-productive.

The Magic Ratio of Positive and Negative Moments, Patsi Krakoff, PhD, www.contentforcoaches-andconsultants.com/the-magic-ratio-of-positive-and-negative-moments/.

The job of the manager/coach is to present his findings in an accurate – but neutral – way. He might say, "Carol, I thought you handled steps 1, 2, and 5 well, but need more help on steps 3 and 4. Let's talk about how you can improve in these two areas."

LEG #3: MOTIVATION – A BUSINESS MODEL

After observation and feedback, we can now move on to the third step: motivation. Motivation is often thought of as "rah, rah" or a wildly enthusiastic "pump 'em up" and "go get 'em" approach. In my experience, this kind of motivation is ultimately unsuccessful because it doesn't provide useful tools to improve your performance.

The most effective motivation comes when both the coach and the person being coached are working in harmony. The salesperson should have well-defined objectives, an effective sales / business plan, and specific targets to shoot for. When these requirements are in place, the trainer / sales coach / sales manager can encourage the salesperson to stay focused on his or her objectives.

What sales trainers have learned is that it is futile to try to encourage someone to do something they don't want to do. The good coach knows that true motivation comes by reminding and encouraging the salesperson to work to achieve agreed-upon goals.

Thus, the effective sales manager / sales coach will motivate a salesperson by working out a follow-up agreement. It will have these parts:

1. A well-defined set of date-sensitive goals, such as: "I will sell 20 units per month, and price my sales to yield a 20% profit margin."
2. Agreed upon record keeping procedures: "I will file sales reports each Monday."
3. Agreed upon follow-up procedures where the sales manager / sales coach regularly talks with the salesperson to discuss how the sales process is working, and to also encourage the salesperson to stay on track to achieve their agreed upon goals.

For example, the sales trainer or coach could say something like, "Carol, the most important thing in your sales activities is to remember to stay focused on your goals on a daily basis. When you think about what you need to do every day, you'll stay on track and have a better chance of achieving your objectives."

What Does Your Sales Training Program Look Like?

IF YOU HAVE:

Observation	√	√	√	
Feedback	√	√		√
Motivation	√		√	√
OUTCOME	Advisor's best chance for sales success.	Less chance of success due to a lack of motivational feedback.	Reduced chance of success: Where is the opportunity for improvement without feedback?	Is feedback valid without observation?

IF YOU HAVE:

Observation	√		
Feedback		√	
Motivation			√
OUTCOME	Not helpful to sales representatives without feedback and motivation.	How valid is feedback if you have not observed sales representative in action?	How useful is motivation without info about salesperson's actions?

The Training Cycle Is Complete

Observation, feedback and motivation – these three steps are needed to produce consistently high levels of production and greater agent retention.

An employer's job is to hire a candidate who meets eligibility and suitability requirements. And if the employer is willing to provide the agent with a consistently applied three-legged sales training program, the agency will enjoy improved agent sales success and improved agent retention.

THREE

Marketing

Ask ten people to describe marketing and you'll get ten different answers. Because it's an imprecise term, it's no surprise that people have a variety of ideas about what marketing means. Some people think successful marketing has to be clever, unusual and esoteric, such as stealth or underground marketing. I don't share this view.

A successful marketing plan simply means that you know your target market and have selected – and use – marketing channels that will put you in front of your ideal prospects on a regular basis. For anyone who's involved in sales in the financial services industry, lack of an effective and sustainable marketing program is the primary source of anxiety. Successful producers are successful marketers. Unsuccessful producers are often good salespeople, but are usually poor or inconsistent marketers.

Marketing Channels – The Roads to Your Clients

Marketing refers to all the activities engaged in prior to the beginning of the sales process. It includes all the activities that will enable you to discover and get in front of a potential prospect (often called a suspect).

Peter Montoya, a marketing and branding expert and owner of Peter Montoya Inc., has identified twenty-two marketing channels available to financial service professionals. According to Montoya, these channels fall into four categories:

Montoya, *The One Year Marketing Plan*, 42-43.

1 Strongly Recommended
2 Sometimes Recommended
3 Rarely Recommended
4 Discouraged

The success of any of these channels depends first upon discovering, and then working with your target market. First, I'll discuss the strongly recommended channels in detail, and then briefly describe channels which generally yield less favorable results. Again, remember that your marketing success increases as you increase your efforts to work with your target market. The goal I stress with all my clients: work with your target market / ideal client 80% of the time.

6 Strongly Recommended Marketing Channels

These channels are based on marketing activities which put you face to face, or live voice to live voice, with anyone who could be a prospect, or could help lead you to meeting with new prospects. Your business brand is based upon selling yourself first, and then your products and services. The best way to do this, since people are ultimately buying you and not a commodity, is to initially make sure that you have personal, warm connections with those who may need your products and services.

For example:

- When you reach prospects and clients on the telephone, that is a warm connection.
- When you send an introductory letter followed up by a phone call, you are seeking a warm connection.
- When you receive an introduction to a prospect from a Center of Influence (see page 41) or a client, that's a warm connection.

If you have formed a network of advisors serving the needs of your target market ("Centers of Service") and a COS sends you a referral, that's a warm connection.

As we're in the personal service business, warm connections are the most effective marketing method available, because serving our clients and customers demands a personal connection. The value of these warm connections cannot be overemphasized.

Out of the twenty-two available marketing channels, these six are *strongly recommended channels.*

STRONGLY RECOMMENDED

1. *Referrals from Clients:* Referrals or introductions from existing clients.
2. *Referrals from Centers of Influence / Professionals:* Referrals are typically CPAs, attorneys, bankers and business managers, but could be anyone who can influence others to talk to you.
3. *Referrals from Centers of Service, Those Vendors Serving the Members of Your Target Market:* Initially you need to discover your target market, and then develop a network of vendors who serve the needs of people in your target market. By managing this network effectively you can build a referral network that yields a continuous supply of high quality referrals. Done right, COS Networking is the most effective marketing channel. *(Key point: A Center of Service does not have to be a traditional Center of Influence.)*

Charles Legalos, PhD, Critical Contacts, Inc.

4. *Special Events:* Take advantage of the opportunity to reinforce connections with existing clients or meet new people in your target market by hosting birthday parties, retirement parties, charity fundraisers and open houses. These events are often described as private – not public – seminars.
5. *Internet Based Communication:* These include your website, emails, newsletters, blogs, pod casts and programs such as LinkedIn and Twitter.
6. *Direct Mail:* Newsletters put your name and ideas in front of your prospect on a regular basis and serve as effective

reminders of your value. Thank you notes and letters are also significant contacts that foster warm relationships.

These six channels require that you have direct contact with the source of the referral and direct contact with the prospect. When you're in direct contact with a potential client, that person can easily determine if they want to do business with you. If you've received a favorable introduction, there is a greater chance of success.

On page 37, I'll show you how you can more easily obtain Client referrals, Centers of Influence referrals, and Centers of Service referrals.

Each of these strongly recommended marketing channels has its own specific requirements. Each channel requires some training, a good deal of focus and attention, and consistent application of specific marketing guidelines. Any of the first six channels can provide, or help provide, a consistent flow of high quality referrals to your target market, as long as you consistently follow the marketing requirements.

Success is not magic; referrals flow from a well-executed marketing program. Only when salespeople falter in executing a good plan do sales results suffer. This brief description of the most important marketing channels looks simple, but simple is not necessarily easy. Effective administration of these marketing channels will determine your level of sales success. The purpose of all of your marketing activities is to do just one thing: put you in a position to start the sales process with a well-qualified suspect who is in your target market.

Risk Avoidance Marketing Channels

The remaining 16 marketing channels may be effective for other businesses, but are not usually the best choices for financial service professionals because they lack a personal connection. See if any of your marketing strategies fall into these categories:

SOMETIMES RECOMMENDED

7 Seminars – Private

8 Indoor Advertising

    a Airport Signage
    b Marquee Advertising

9 Outdoor Advertising
    a Billboards
    b Building Signage
    c Bus Benches / Boards

10 Point-of-Purchase Display
    a Banners
    b Counter Displays
    c Mobiles
    d Multi-Media CD-ROM
    e Shopping Carts

11 Telemarketing
    a Outbound
    b On-Hold Narration
    c Conference Calls
    d Teleseminars
    e Fax Blasting

12 Trade Shows

13 Sponsorships (usually sporting events)

RARELY RECOMMENDED

14 Canvassing / Cold Calls

15 Seminars – Public (you know – the free dinner approaches)

16 Public Relations
    a Magazine / Newspaper Articles
    b Radio and TV Commentary
    c Print Feature Stories

17 Radio Advertising
    a Host-Paid Radio Show
    b Commercials
    c Infomercials

18 Print Advertising

  - a Display Advertising
  - b Classified Advertising
  - c Yellow Pages
  - d Inserts / Circulars

DISCOURAGED

19 Buzz Marketing

20 Publishing
  - a Books
  - b Paid Newsletters

21 Television Advertising
  - a Host-Paid TV Show
  - b Pay-for-Guest TV Show
  - c Commercials
  - d Infomercials

22 Cinema Advertising
  - a Movie Trailer Ads
  - b Pre-Movie Advertising Slides

Some financial service professionals are drawn to marketing activities that have the lure of producing good results while avoiding personal rejection. Public seminars, for example, are energy-, time- and money-intensive activities that sometimes produce good results (if you seek out warm connections). But they don't initially require you to make a personal, warm connection.

Some advisors conduct educational seminars offering free advice about financial services. This is another method of attempting to get people to meet you while reducing the initial risk of any personal rejection. There is even less chance for rejection in newspaper, radio or TV advertising, and public relations campaigns. Each of these activities can produce favorable results in terms of name recognition and goodwill in the community, but they all involve a good deal of time and money. In my experience, these methods are no more effective than engaging in simple, warm marketing programs – the six strongly recommended channels mentioned above.

A Closer Look at Referrals

Without a doubt, referrals are at the core of effective marketing activities. As previously mentioned, the best referrals can come from 3 basic sources: Clients, Centers of Influence, or Centers of Service.

Each of these three marketing channels has specific requirements. For example, asking for client referrals involves a good deal more than just asking clients or prospects for the names of other people that you can talk to. In fact, there are 10 steps needed to have a continuous supply of referrals.

See the *10 Steps to Building a Referred Lead Engine* workbook at SalesSolutionsPress.com.

In order to achieve your overall marketing goals, the most difficult task is obtaining referrals on a consistent basis. Cerulli Associates has stated that only 11% of financial advisors ask for referrals on a regular basis. Why is this number so low? Compare the selling process with the marketing or referral process, and you'll notice that when you make a sale you have followed a well organized process. You also know that not everybody will buy from you (the average is about one out of three). Emotionally, you're prepared for the "no," which makes the one out of three ratio acceptable. As you know, salespeople thrive on intermittent gratification.

Asking for referrals, on the other hand, does not always follow such an organized path. If you use the "I get paid in two ways" approach, or the simpler "Who do you know that I should talk to?" method, you often get poor results. How do you feel when you ask for a referral in this way, and the response is, "I don't know anybody"? Too often you do not know a good response to this reply and may feel embarrassed. I remember one sales agent I coached saying he felt like a beggar when asking for referrals. Nobody likes to feel that way; it's easy to see why so few advisors regularly ask for referrals, especially if their prospecting methods consistently yield rejection and poor results.

Without a workable marketing plan, it's no surprise that financial advisors worry about the timing of their next sale. Fortunately, there is a system available which can help you overcome most of the difficulties connected with obtaining client referrals.

How to Create a Client Referral System

Available at coachnickray.com.

A proven client referral system is described in my workbook, *10 Steps to Building a Referred Lead Engine*.

The title says a great deal because it outlines an organic and natural system for obtaining a continuous flow of high-quality referrals. Out of the 10 steps, the three most important ones are used below. For simplicity, I will label them here as Steps 1, 2, 3.

CLIENT REFERRAL SYSTEM STEP 1 – INTENTION

Intention is making the decision to discover your target market and to prospect on a regular basis in your target market. No objective is ever achieved without having the intention to do it. Assume that you intend to prospect and market your services on a regular basis. This intention continuously fuels your motivation, because intention determines attention. In other words, what you intend to do will determine what you pay attention to and what you will do.

CLIENT REFERRAL SYSTEM STEP 2 – USE A PRINTED FACT FINDER

You will be your most productive if you use a printed fact finder. This is the key to effective selling and prospecting. Using a printed fact finder will help you achieve these basic objectives:

- *What* is important to your client – and what benefits your client hopes to get by working with you.
- *Who* is important to your client – these are future prospects.
- The level of satisfaction your client has with his professional advisors – these can become Centers of Influence.
- Psychographic and demographic information about your clients and prospects – this information helps you refine your target market.

Fact finders will be discussed in depth in Chapter Seven.

Obtaining vitally important client information on a regular basis will help you become a more effective salesperson and a better marketer.

CLIENT REFERRAL SYSTEM STEP 3 – HOW TO ASK FOR REFERRALS

My experience is that most people who buy from you, and stay with you, are satisfied with your products and services. Starting from this positive assumption, here is an easy process you can use to obtain referrals or introductions.

- Begin the referral conversation by saying something like this: "Jess, I want to have a brief conversation with you about how I can help other people that you know and care about. I'm wondering if I can put you on the spot for just a minute. Could you give me a brief evaluation of how you feel about the value of the products and services that I provide for you?" Wait for the response, and when the response is positive – and it is 80-90% of the time – you move to:
- Affirm the positive feedback. "Great. I'm happy that you feel that way. You know, my purpose of being in business is to help my clients achieve their most important goals and feel good about the results." You then quickly transition to:
- "What I'd like to do is be able to provide the same level and quality of service I've provided you, to people you know and care about."
- "I'm wondering if we could talk about this for just a few minutes. Would it be OK with you if we had a brief conversation?" On the assumption that your client is satisfied with the service you've provided (and they are almost all of the time), the typical referrer will say, "Sure, I'd be happy to talk with you."

Now is the time when the "capturing names" part of your fact-finding process pays off. If you've done a good job of completing your fact finder, you've probably captured the names of six, eight, or ten people who are important to your client. You then say, "You know Jess, you mentioned a good friend of yours, Mary Jones. I was thinking of calling her, but I don't know too much about her. Do you think there's a good fit between Mary and me? Do you think she would appreciate the kind of services that I provide?"

You repeat this process as you inquire about each person whose name you captured. As you feed these "captured" names from the fact finder, you make it much easier to obtain a referral. Use this prospecting system regularly, and you'll get the referrals you need. Please notice this process requires that *you* do most of the work by feeding your client the names of people you'd like to talk to. As you continue to work in your target market, you'll notice you receive referrals to others who are in your target market as well (because most referrals are lateral).

Types of Client Referrals

This system for obtaining client referrals is easy to implement so long as you have, and use, a good printed fact finder when you are gathering prospect / client information. As mentioned above, a good fact finder will make it easy for you to collect four types of information:

1 Client needs (what's important)

2 Key people in your client's life (who's important)

3 Key advisors, and how your client feels about these advisors (potential Centers of Influence)

4 Key data about your client's life (improves your target market information)

If you fail to use a printed fact finder to capture names, it makes it harder to "prime the pump" when having a referral conversation. How many times have you received the following response when asking for referrals? "I really don't know anybody that needs your services." Your inner thoughts are that your client is a successful person and probably knows 200 people. Is it possible that out of these 200 people, your client doesn't know a single person who could benefit by your services? That's absurd isn't it? The key is for you to do your job well by making it easy for your client to refer you to people they know: feeding names captured in your printed fact finder is the easiest way to do this.

Remember These Steps

Here's a summary of the key steps from "*10 Steps to Building a Referred Lead Engine.*"

- Have the intention to regularly obtain referrals to people in your target market.
- Use a printed fact finder on a regular basis to capture names of future referrals, preferably in your target market.
- Use the 4-step inquiry process to obtain referrals.

How to Develop Profitable Center of Influence Relationships

The second strongly recommended marketing channel is obtaining referrals from your Centers of Influence. By using the process described below, you'll be able to develop effective Center of Influence relationships.

STEP 1 – DETERMINE CHEMISTRY: Is there good chemistry between you and the potential Center of Influence? I don't give referrals to people I don't like and I suspect that you don't either. When attempting to develop a Center of Influence relationship, first determine if good chemistry exists. Then work to build a continuing relationship by following the steps below. If there is not good chemistry – accept that it's unlikely that you will ever get business from this person. No matter how nice a person you are, how competent and professional you are, not everyone is going to like you. Recognize that chemistry, or the lack of chemistry, is something you can't control. If it's absent – move on.

STEP 2 – DETERMINE TARGET MARKET OVERLAP: Is the Center of Influence working in your target market? This is an important point – because your best referrals are to people in your target market. Question: Do you know what your target market is? Do you know the Center of Influence's target market? Are you and the Center of Influence working in the *same* target market? This is an important requirement for building a lasting, productive relationship. Referrals to target market prospects will allow you to bring your special skills to those who will appreciate you most.

STEP 3 – DETERMINE REFERRAL POTENTIAL: Does the Center of Influence give referrals? Even when good chemistry exists, and you and the Center of Influence are in the same target market, unwillingness to give referrals will always lead to an unproductive relationship. If this situation occurs, thank the Center of Influence for his time, and search elsewhere for your ideal Center of Influence.

STEP 4 – MEET REGULARLY: Will this Center of Influence meet with you on a regular basis? The purpose of these meetings is for you to provide something of value so that this advisor directly benefits by meeting with you. Regular meetings also confirm that you are trustworthy and reliable. The best value you can bring to a Center of Influence is a referral. Whether you bring a referral or not, a basic guideline for Centers of Influence meetings is to follow a GAP agenda: Goals, Achievements, Problems. Each meeting should be GAP based, and not just a drop-in call to say hello. Most people are too busy to waste time on purely social calls.

STEP 5 – RECIPROCATION: If the Center of Influence will meet with you on a regular basis, is in your target market, will give referrals, and has good chemistry with you, will this person agree to send you at least one person to talk with in the next twelve months? You waste a valuable asset (you!) when you send referrals to people who don't reciprocate. By providing value to the Center of Influence at each meeting, it is reasonable to expect that you'll get business in return. Sound business practices require balance in the relationship.

A surprising fact is that you only need six to ten Centers of Influence in your target market to provide you with a continuous flow of high quality referrals. It may take 12 to 18 months to find and meet with the Centers of Influence before they send you business. You should have a well thought out marketing plan that you implement on a regular basis. You can learn the complete system in my workbook, "*Developing a Center of Influence Engine – The Relationship System.*"

Available at coachnickray.com.

How to Develop Centers of Service in Your Target Market

The third strongly recommended marketing channel is to develop and manage Centers of Service. Centers of Service are vendors serving the members of your target market. Charles Legalos, PhD, the founder and creator of Critical Contacts Inc., a management and marketing consulting company, developed a system which helps people build networks that provide referrals on a continuous basis. The process has these basic steps:

For more information see criticalcontacts.com.

1. Discover your target market and the ideal client in your target market.
2. Discover the watering holes and hangouts where your target market members meet (places where people need to go for important business information).
3. Discover the access you have to your target market at their watering holes.
4. Develop and manage a small network of vendors serving the needs of the members of your target market.

By following this target market based networking program, advisors have been able to reduce their marketing efforts by as much as 50%-80% and still obtain a consistent level of high quality referrals. Conclusion: Development of a small network of vendors serving your target market is usually sufficient to build a very profitable practice.

Why Don't We Work with Our Ideal Clients?

Most of us should work with ideal clients at least 80% of the time. Ideal client relationships are easier, more fun and more profitable than selling to just anyone who will talk to us.

This being so, why do most of us work with ideal clients less often than we'd like to? There are four basic reasons why we don't achieve this 80% goal:

1. We don't know how to discover (or uncover) our target market.
2. We think we choose our target market – but we don't – our target market chooses us.

3. We haven't implemented a marketing plan to regularly get us in front of our target market.
4. We have not identified our ideal client – the actual type of person who works in our target market, and whom we have identified as a person who chooses to work with us.

Discover Your Target Market

One of the mistaken notions about target marketing is that you choose your target market. Perhaps you or your manager decided it was time to upgrade your market – to go where the high income folks live. Perhaps you decided you wanted to specialize in small businesses or professionals (CPAs, doctors, attorneys). Whatever your choice, how successful have you been?

Some people do succeed in working in a target market of their choosing. Many do not. Even though I know nothing about your practice, my guess is that you do not work in your target market 80% of the time. I have one simple test: do you successfully and consistently close more than 35% of your cases? Industry averages are that about 1/3 of all sales presentations generate a sale. If you do not close 50-60% of your cases, you are not talking to enough of the right people in the first place.

The initial source of this closing ratio information came from a long-term study conducted by Al Granum, now a retired Chicago, Illinois, Northwestern Mutual Life General Agent. Here is the story:

The senior agents in Granum's Chicago agency regularly asserted that they were better closers, and better salespeople, than the rookies. Granum actually didn't know if this claim was true, nor could the experienced agents prove their claim. Al decided to keep records. He simply asked each agent to record his or her sales activities as follows: number of referrals, number of cases opened, and number of sales.

At a meeting I attended where Granum spoke, here is what he reported: After many years of record keeping, the results were interesting – and quite surprising:

111,000 referrals

33,000 opened cases

11,000 sales

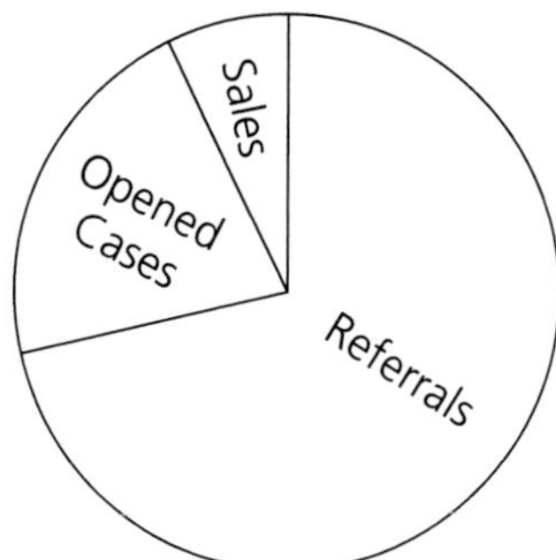

10-3-1. This ratio held regardless of the agent's experience level. One obvious conclusion is that consistent marketing activity is the number 1 activity required to produce a consistent level of sales. No one is immune from this basic requirement. Another interesting fact is that even the most experienced and most successful agents still only sold to about 1/3 of the people they saw. Their sales experience was and is largely irrelevant because of one basic fact:

The *buyer* makes the decision as to whom he will buy from. All the desire in the world that you have to make a sale won't make someone buy from you. That is why we have to see so many people – 2/3 won't buy from us. These ratios hold because we don't know who our target market is, and thus we maintain high activity to compensate for the fact that we are not talking to our target market 80% of the time.

Occasionally, a salesperson will begin working in his target market more consistently. In this case, sales performance will improve. People working in their natural market close more than 50% of their cases.

Working in Your Target Market

Even the best salespeople typically take at least ten years to discover their target market. It may even take 20-30 years because, in most cases, working in your target market was accidental, not intentional, and didn't happen by conscious design.

Is there a way to work in your target market 80% of the time? Yes – but you must carefully follow these 3 steps to discover your target market.

Available at SalesSolutionsPress.com.

1 Complete the *Invisible Market Matrix (IMM)* to discover the defining characteristics of your target market and the specific characteristics of your ideal client.

2 Discover how well you and your target market are in alignment.

See sample referral logs in Appendix 2 on page 144.

3 Use referral logs to determine how consistently you give referrals to, and receive referrals from, your target market.

Use of these three tools will allow you to discover your target market, and how frequently you work in your target market. Your target market is a blend of those who have chosen to work with you and how well your own personal interests match those of your target market.

The outcome of this three-part investigation will yield a target market made of people who like you *and* whom you like. I think you'll agree that it's a lot more fun to work with your favorite clients. Completing the three-part target market discovery process will yield important and useful marketing information.

How You Can Use Your Target Market Information

BETTER CLIENT REFERRALS

You can use the description of your target market/ideal client profile to help you prospect more effectively with your existing clients. This simple step will increase your effectiveness, because you'll ask your clients for referrals to people who meet your target market/ideal client definition (client referrals).

BETTER CENTER OF INFLUENCE REFERRALS

You can also use target market information to develop a more effective relationship with your Centers of Influence, by encouraging these Centers to send you referrals to members of your target market.

Knowing that you want to give – and receive – referrals to members of your target market will enable you to be more selective when seeking and giving referrals.

BETTER NETWORK REFERRALS

You can also seek out those places where there is a concentration of members of your target market. We call these places watering holes. By simply showing up at the watering hole on a regular basis, and giving to the organization (volunteer for committee work, speak and provide articles to their organization's magazine or newsletter) you will, within 6-9 months, begin to receive business from members of the organization serving your target market.

Attending Watering Holes

One caveat: *Never, never* talk about your business at an organization meeting. If you receive a request for information, ask to speak about your services away from the meeting at a later date. Violate this rule, and little or no business will come your way, for if you talk about your business at an organization meeting, organization members will think you only come to meetings to get business. This attitude is generally not well received.

By attending your target market organization meetings on a regular basis, you can also begin to develop a network of vendors serving the needs of the members of your target market. Then, by meeting with these vendors on a quarterly basis and working to bring value and referrals to them, you'll build a network of people working in and serving your target market. This is the definition of an effective network: vendors serving the needs of the members of your target market. These vendors are called Centers of Service.

See the *Invisible Market Matrix* at SalesSolutionsPress.com to find your natural target market.

Target marketing – it takes a little time to discover your target market, but it's worth a fortune in the long run.

Marketing Highlights

- ❖ Discover your target market / ideal client profile.
- ❖ Define your product offering – what benefits do you provide?
- ❖ Use at least 2 or 3 strongly recommended marketing channels on a regular basis.
- ❖ Create a written marketing plan.
- ❖ Create specific marketing objectives (number of referrals, number of client contacts, number of meetings).
- ❖ Keep records of your marketing activity.
- ❖ Create uniform marketing materials – letterhead, business cards, brochures, etc.
- ❖ Develop a website.
- ❖ Continuously improve your referral activities.

The tools described in this chapter will not completely eliminate all your marketing difficulties, but they will make your business life easier. In the next chapter we will explore ways to measure the effectiveness of using these marketing strategies.

FOUR

Measuring Marketing Effectiveness

Do you have measurable marketing objectives? Do you know how many referrals you need on a weekly or monthly basis? Do you know how many cases you need to open in order to meet your sales objectives? Do you know how many cases you have to successfully close to meet your sales objectives? Does your marketing plan include regular contact with your existing clients? Do you have this system automated?

To determine your sales objectives, it's important to look at your sales process to see how it is linked to your marketing program.

The Sales Process Overview

- Establish and maintain marketing activities
- Opening the case
- Completing the fact finder
- Preparing and presenting your sales proposal
- Closing the case / getting paid
- Delivering the case – establishing and cementing the relationship
- Maintaining administrative processes, client records, meeting compliance requirements, and maintaining ongoing client contact

Please rank these marketing / sales activities in two basic ways: in terms of importance in the sales process, and in percentage of time spent on each activity.

"Your Rank of Importance" indicates the way you rank the importance of your marketing and sales activities.

NICK RAY'S RANK OF IMPORTANCE	SALES FUNCTION	YOUR RANK OF IMPORTANCE	% OF WORK TIME SPENT IN EACH SALES FUNCTION
1	Closing the case / getting paid		
2	Maintaining marketing activities		
3	Completing the fact finder		
4	Opening the case		
5	Preparing and presenting your sales proposal		
6	Delivering the case		
7	Maintaining administrative processes, client records, and meeting compliance requirements		

What's Most Important?

You'll notice that closing the sale and getting paid is priority number 1. Many people are surprised by this ranking, but the bottom line is the bottom line. Any business, in order to succeed and sustain itself, must be profitable. No matter how good you are at every other aspect of the sales process, you must successfully close a sufficient number of cases *and* get paid to stay in business.

A successful financial advisor or salesperson must be consistent in managing his/her practice to achieve profitability objectives. The difference between a great salesperson and a great business person is the ability to run a profitable business. Great business people meet their sales goals *and* their profit goals.

See "The Breakeven Budget" at SalesSolutionPress.com.

The Basic Cause of Uneven Sales Activity

It is important to recognize that the biggest single cause of uneven or inconsistent income is the lack of consistent marketing activity.

Here is a typical sales situation: You have been active in marketing your services and you've gotten very busy. You've opened many cases, have much proposal work to do, many presentations to make and cases to close. Somehow you forget to maintain a regular, consistent marketing effort. Just about the time all of your cases are completed and you've been paid, you discover (surprise!) that you don't have enough cases in the pipeline.

What was the problem? Perhaps you thought that there was a correlation between your current marketing efforts and current sales success. Unconsciously, you may have thought that making a sale relieved you of any current marketing requirements.

The reality is that the sale you made today is the result of what you did yesterday, just as every sale you make tomorrow will be the result of what you do today. In fact, there is *no* correlation between a current sale and your current marketing activities. This is the mistake made by every salesperson suffering from uneven production.

The solution is simple. Arrange your schedule to ensure that your marketing activities are regular and consistent. Never allow yourself to be so busy that you don't do your required daily/weekly marketing activities. The most successful producers have discovered that regular marketing activity is absolutely critical to having consistent production. If you forget this – and most of us have – you'll soon experience the stress that comes from uneven production.

An example: I have a client whom I'll call Henry. He is a very successful producer, well organized and very consistent. We were recently talking, when he lamented the fact that he hadn't opened up many new cases. I asked what he thought the problem was, and he said that he'd been so busy that he had failed to make his marketing phone calls.

What's interesting is that while Henry works forty-five or fifty hours a week, his phoning activity takes at most five or six hours a week. Phoning is a very high leverage activity because about 10% of his working time is responsible for at least 50% or 60% of his income.

When Henry realized this fact, he made one simple decision: to make his calls each week at the same time, and to forbid non-emergency interruptions. Henry was well organized and had enough prospects in the pipeline that consistent Tuesday morning marketing calls eliminated almost all of the ups and downs in his practice.

This is a fact of life that applies to all salespeople in all industries. Your challenge: to discover when to schedule your marketing activities, and to carry them out on a regular basis. Some may consider that following this advice will result in a boring practice – but it's also advice that, if followed, may produce a boring but consistently good income.

Your Personalized Marketing Plan Objective

The basic objective of a marketing plan is to get you in front of your ideal clients at least 80% of the time. The only way to tell if you are achieving this goal is to keep accurate sales activity records. No business that's well run operates without the periodic evaluation of its marketing efforts. If you ask any effective business owner, they will be able to tell you their sales and profit margins. The same accountability standards apply to the financial services business as well. If your records do not help you evaluate your business success, consider using the following simple model.

CAPS: A Tool to Help You Analyze Your Marketing Effectiveness

MONTH____ YR______

E-Marketing Process→ Sales Process→

RECOMMENDED REFERRAL SOURCE	# OF REFERRALS RECEIVED	CONTACTS MADE	APPOINTMENTS MADE & KEPT	PRESENTATIONS MADE	SALES MADE
From Clients					
From Centers of Influence					
From Centers of Service					
From Direct Mail					
From Call-Ins					
From All Other Sources					

"CAPS" available at SalesSolutionsPress.com.

DEFINITION OF REFERRAL SOURCES

CLIENT: someone who has purchased something from you and uses your services exclusively.

COI: A professional who can influence a person to see you.

COS: Anyone serving the needs of your target market who can recommend you to members of that target market (does *not* have to be a Center of Influence).

HOW TO USE THIS CHART

Simply make a hash mark (/) for each activity. Make one hash mark for each referral received, and placed in it the correct referral source box. Keep your records daily and analyze these records monthly. Your goal is to determine how well each of your marketing channels is working. Use these records to help you determine: an automated CAPS program is available from my website.

- If you are receiving enough referrals to achieve your income goals
- Your sale ratios for each marketing channel
- How to use these sales ratios to help you improve your marketing effectiveness

Mike Jay, business coach and founder of B\COACH, a business coaching school, gets credit for this idea.

After you have used the CAPS forms to record and analyze your sales activities, you will be able to accurately calculate the number of referrals you will need to meet your financial objectives.

Next you'll need to select the marketing channels you're going to use. How many referrals will you need from each of the marketing channels you've selected? The standard formula is 10-3-1: 10 referred leads, 3 presentations made, 1 sale. (Your numbers may vary.)

By knowing your financial objectives, and by analyzing your selected marketing channels, you will be able to establish a regular schedule for your marketing activities and to set appropriate marketing goals. As our client Henry discovered, he needed to schedule calling activities four or five hours per week. He knew this effort was required for him to achieve his annual sales goals. He now schedules from 8 a.m. until noon on Tuesdays to do this. Henry also knows his target market / ideal client profile and how many referrals he must obtain to generate the weekly appointments needed to achieve his selling activity goals.

Assessing Your Marketing Plan

Do you have a written marketing program?

Do you have an identifiable target market? (Your target market is made up of people who have chosen to do business with you. You don't choose your target market; it chooses you.)

Do you have specific marketing objectives, such as number of referrals, number of new cases per month?

Are your referral objectives broken down into selected marketing channels?

Do you record your marketing activities on a daily basis (CAPS)?

Do you analyze your marketing activities at least monthly?

Do all of your print materials (business cards, presentation pages, letterhead, etc.) have a consistent look?

Has all of your printed material been approved by your compliance department?

Do you have an up-to-date website?

Do you regularly use LinkedIn or Twitter?

Do you have a written marketing program which schedules regular contact with your clients and prospects?

Have you asked your best clients for a description of the benefits your services provide (your value propositions)?

Is your product offering well defined?

Do you consistently work in your target market (goal: 80%)?

What conclusions have you come to about your marketing program?

Your Marketing Plan Assignment

- Describe your product offering.
- Discover your target market / ideal client profile.
- Discover your value propositions.
- Produce a written marketing plan.
- Make sure your marketing material has a consistent look and is compliance approved.
- Determine the number of referrals you need per week from each of your marketing channels.
- Calendar your marketing activities at least one week in advance.
- Record your CAPS record information daily; analyze monthly.

Benefits of Completing Your Marketing / Sales Evaluation Process

You'll determine if you're meeting your marketing / sales objectives. If you're not, you'll have enough specific data to help you select the changes you should make. If, for example, you don't have enough prospects to talk to, perhaps you need to start using a printed fact finder to capture names of future referrals. You may also need to add additional strongly recommended marketing channels. If you'd like to work in a target market and get referrals from others working in that same target market, you'll need to discover and implement a system to work with Centers of Service in your target market (the network method).

Tools to Help You Improve Your Marketing Success

Each of the three highly recommended marketing channels listed below is a complete system. While the goal of each of these marketing channels is to produce a consistent flow of high quality referrals, the channels are very different in operation.

I've created each of the following tools to help you maneuver through these marketing channels. The first two are workbooks and the third is a software program. All three are available at SalesSolutions Press.com.

1. *10 Steps to Building a Referred Lead Engine*
2. *Building a Center of Influence Engine – The Relationship System*
3. The *Invisible Market Matrix* software helps you discover your natural target market and ideal client profile.

Available at SalesSolutionsPress.com.

Dealing with Reluctance to Have a Referral Conversation

There's always a certain amount of risk involved in selling. Whenever you ask someone to spend money, there's the risk of them saying no. The financial services business is built on obtaining referrals to maintain sales, which, like all sales efforts, carries the risk of rejection. A regular built-in process for obtaining new people to talk to is mandatory to keep your pipeline filled with future prospects. When you accept this reality, you will also come to accept that you will not always receive a "yes" when asking for the sale, nor will you always receive a "yes" when asking for referrals. This is a fact of life for any salesperson, and when you accept it, you'll design your marketing program to allow for the inevitable "no" factor, which is inevitable. Regular marketing activity reduces the sting of getting a "no" when asking for referrals for these reasons:

- You'll never be overly dependent on a limited number of referral sources.
- You'll always be getting the referrals you need because you ask the right people often enough.
- Regular prospecting helps you become more effective having referral conversations.

Personal Branding

An issue that is relatively recent in financial services activities is personal, or practice, branding. Branding is a well-established activity in larger companies. Branding in large-scale business activities is both an issue of identity and a guarantee of quality. Well-known brands – such as BMW, Mercedes, Cadillac, Cartier, Tiffany, Rolex and Movado – have identifiable characteristics and offer a particular benefit to the buyer. To the extent that appearance, or image, is important, a brand's reputation is especially important – important enough for people to pay extra to buy the product.

A brand also carries with it a guarantee of quality. Buyers come to depend on a company that has built a solid reputation for providing good products and good service. In fact, customers will often pay a premium for superior service. Consider the personal computer. As many of you know, it is possible to buy a first-rate, but unknown, computer brand for far less than you'd pay for a well-known brand. Yet the typical customer would not buy an unknown product for the simple reason that no quality guarantee exists. Thus, a brand is not only an identifying mark or image, but also represents a guarantee of quality that will protect the customer if a quality or service problem should arise.

A brand, then, is the *culmination* of a process of building a recognizable identity for a product or service. The brand represents a value people will pay for and a product to which the buyer will remain loyal. Consider:

- BMW – The Ultimate Driving Machine
- FedEx – The World On Time
- Target – Expect More
- Nike – Just Do It.

Of significance is that the brand has value if it has earned the right. Branding activity, no matter how well done, does not automatically confer loyalty or trust, even if the brand is widely recognized. The GM and Chrysler brands represent companies which are extremely well known – but whose customers are no longer as loyal as they were in the past.

If you decide to engage in the branding process, these basic requirements should be met:

- Discover your target market profile.
- Define your ideal client within your target market.
- Be able to provide value propositions regarding your products and services.
- Be able to provide a clearly defined description of the products or services you offer.
- Have a well-defined geographical area you serve.
- Create an 8-10 word phrase or slogan describing what you do and who you are.

The issues described above provide the foundation for the development of your brand. An effective brand is the essence of the products and services you provide to your clients. A brand is not something you paste onto what you do; it is an accurate description of what you have already done – and what your customers and clients can expect from you when they do business with you in the future.

For further information on marketing, see *The Brand Called You* by Peter Montoya.

The Three Elements of Your Brand

1. Your Company Name
   Your company name makes you findable and referable.
   It differentiates you from others and provides a clear and positive perception of who you are.
2. Your Slogan
   Ten words or less; your slogan should transmit who you are, what you do and the benefits you provide to your target market.
3. Your Icon
   An icon is a graphic symbol that amplifies your identity. Your icon is the most easily recognizable part of your brand identity.

Your Identity Package

Your slogan not only communicates your services and the benefits you provide to your target market; it also serves as a visual mark that binds all your printed material together. Use your logo consistently to demonstrate your quality and professionalism.

Cohesive Marketing Material

FIVE

Opening the Case

Your marketing efforts have yielded referrals; your next task is to determine if your suspect (the person you've been referred to) is a prospect. A suspect is simply a person whom you think *may* be a buyer of your products or services. When you conduct an initial interview (opening the case), your goal is to discover three things:

1. Is the suspect a prospect (prospect = buyer)?
2. If so, is she a prospect for *you*?
3. Is your suspect motivated to solve his problems at this time?

Opening the Case Assessment

Do you have standard language for requesting an initial interview appointment?

What is your exit strategy if the answer to #1 is no?

What are your objectives for the initial interview appointment?

Do you have an agenda format for the initial interview?

How often do you use a printed agenda?

Please list some of the benefits your services provide to your clients.

Do you have an initial interview questionnaire?

How often do you ask your referral sources to pave the way for your introductory call (send a letter, email, fax, personal introduction, etc)?

Describe your exit strategy when the suspect remains a suspect, or is not a prospect for you – and the sales process has ended.

Sales Stages: From Suspect to Advocate

There are certain stages that occur naturally during the sales process. Learning to recognize each stage can help you determine whether or not a referral will become not only someone who buys your products, but one who champions your services by recommending you to others.

Stage 1 Suspect

Stage 2 Prospect

Stage 3 Customer

Stage 4 Client

Stage 5 Advocate

STAGE 1

A *suspect* is a referral, or anyone who may become a buyer. We don't know the outcome at this stage, but you *suspect* the person may be interested in your products or services.

STAGE 2

A *prospect* is a suspect who has expressed a specific interest in taking action – with someone – towards buying the products or services that are being offered.

STAGE 3

The third stage occurs when the prospect becomes a buyer, or customer, for *your* services. A *customer* is one who will buy from you – but not necessarily on an exclusive basis.

STAGE 4

A *client* is a customer who buys your product or services *exclusively from you.*

STAGE 5

The final category is an *advocate*. An advocate is a person who has bought something from you and is someone who will sing your praises to other potential buyers. An advocate is someone who will say to a referral, "You know, Joe is a terrific person. You ought to talk to him about the kind of services that he offers." While typically a client, an advocate may just be a customer.

The Sales Process

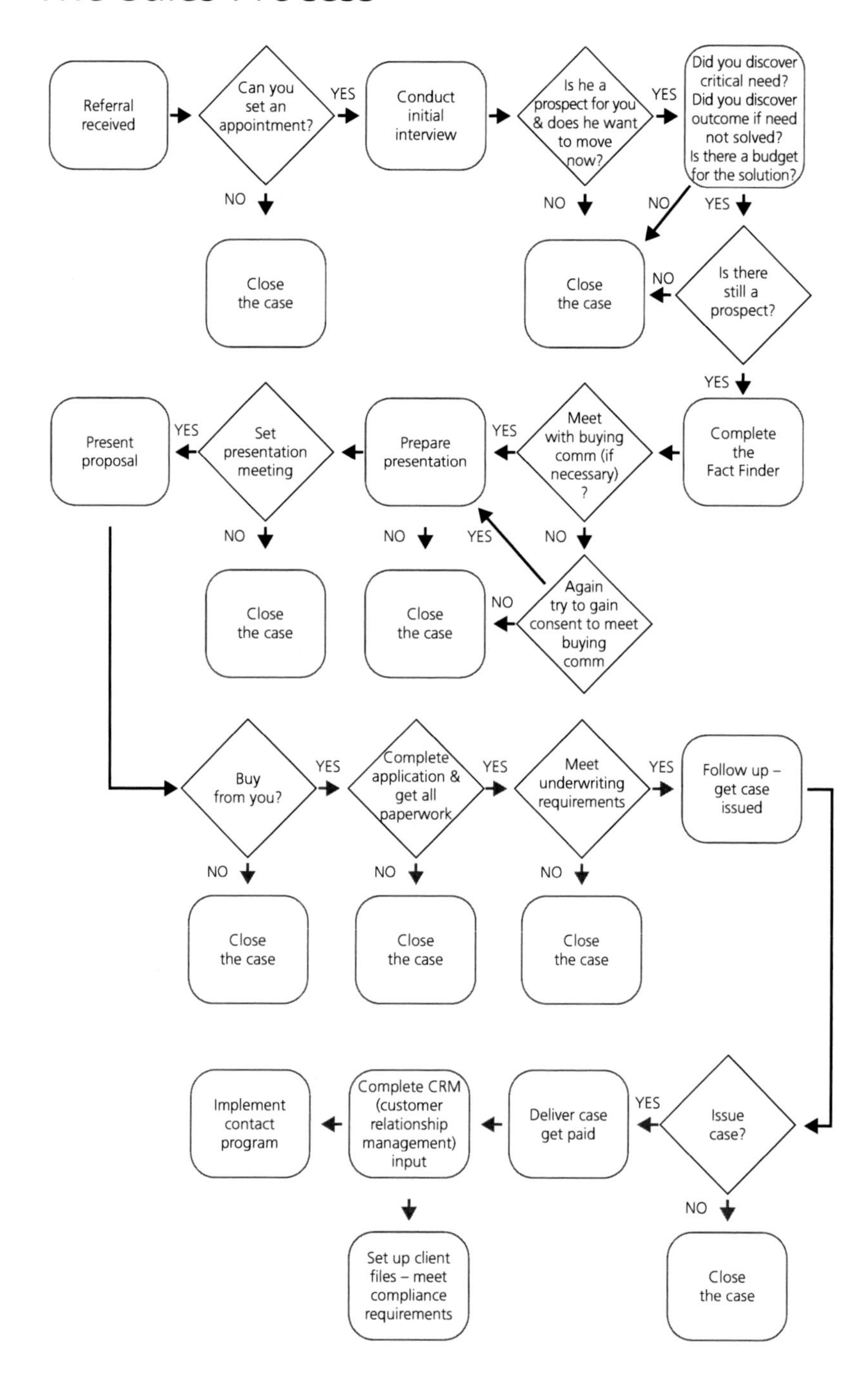

The Referral Call

The purpose of the referral call is to take the first step toward determining whether a suspect will become a prospect.

First, Obtain an Interview

Your first contact with the referral is typically a telephone conversation. Before you make the phone call you must have a very clear idea of your objective. It's simply to obtain an interview with the referral. It is not to extol the virtues of your wares. It is not to convince the potential buyer how fabulous you are or how wonderful your product is. It's not to explain in great detail what you do. It's much simpler: It's to obtain an appointment to meet.

Step 1 State your name
Step 2 Briefly describe what you do
Step 3 Mention the referrer's name
Step 4 State the purpose for your call
Step 5 Ask for the appointment

A Sample Telephone Conversation

"Hello Jess. My name is Nick Ray and I'm in the financial advisory business. My client and your friend, Ellen Smith, gave me your name. The reason for my call is very simple. Ellen thought that we might work well together and suggested that we have a fifteen or twenty minute initial interview. With this thought in mind, could we get together next Tuesday at 2:00 PM or next Thursday at 3:00 PM?"

Please notice that the only purpose of your call is to obtain an appointment. Be brief and stay focused on setting an appointment. If the referral has any interest in what you have to offer, the mention of the referrer's name and the services you provide should help you gain consent to set up an initial appointment. That is the objective of your call.

Expanding on the Purpose of Your Call

As you are explaining why you're calling, you could add something like: "Jess, the purpose for our meeting is to discover three things. One, whether you have an actual need for my services; two, to discover if we could work well together; and three, if this is the right time for you to move forward. Ellen didn't say anything about your particular needs; all she said was she thought we might work well together. With those thoughts in mind, can we meet next week? Say, Tuesday or Thursday?"

Let us assume that you have gotten an affirmative response: set the appointment, say thank you and say, "I'll see you next Tuesday, the 5th, at your office at 1:30 pm. Let me confirm your address: It's 1234 Main Street, right? Great, see you next week."

Dealing with Objections when Setting an Appointment

I operate under a simple principle: I don't go where I'm not invited. That's why I limit dealing with objections to one or, at most, two attempts. If you find yourself getting appointments with fewer than 50% of your referrals, you need to look at the underlying reasons. Typical reasons include:

- Referrals are not in your target market.
- The referral is not from a strong referror.
- The referral is cold – too much time has passed since getting the referral.
- The referror did not set up your call by letting the referral know you would call.
- You did not adequately qualify the referral in the first place.

The Sales Activity Your Call Provides

Assume that we operate on the 10-3-1 principle:

My experience is that if you have ten good referrals, you will be able to set about three to five initial interview appointments. If the quality of the referrals is strong, you will have better results; that's why referrals from your best clients are preferred. The best way to have strong referrals is to have the referrer call, e-mail, use LinkedIn, text message, or personally introduce you to the referral. The more you can encourage the referrer to be an advocate for you, the more likely an appointment will follow.

Have Realistic Sales Expectations

You'll never get appointments with everybody you call, nor will you sell everybody you see. Having this perspective eases the pressure of trying to turn every referred call lead into an appointment. It also emphasizes that you have to make sure that your pipeline is consistently filled with attractive candidates.

As mentioned in the marketing section, having too few ideal clients to talk to is a problem many advisors face. Rather than worrying about having the best sales pitch, it's much more important to have enough people to talk to. Your success rate will also go up if you are dealing with people in your target market, as you'll probably have the most expertise for those prospects who match your target market/ideal client profile. Buyers want, more than anything, an advisor who understands their particular circumstances and can help them solve their problems. The more you specialize, the more experience and expertise you'll acquire, will make you more attractive to your ideal clients.

The Initial Interview

You've achieved your objective, which was to get an appointment. What do you do during the appointment to effectively utilize your fifteen or twenty minutes?

Remember: we have only three objectives in mind. First, to discover if there's good chemistry between you and your suspect. You don't have to do anything special; all you have to do is talk to the person – you'll easily discover if there's good chemistry.

The second goal, however, is to determine if the suspect is actually a prospect. This can be a little more complicated. Essentially, your services or products have to provide a *solution to the problem* that your prospect or suspect actually has at the moment.

Third, your suspect has to have a problem that he wants to solve *now*. Having a problem that he wants to deal with in six months or a year may give you a *future* prospect, but it doesn't give you a *current* prospect. In the initial interview you're discovering, and that's the key word, whether or not the prospect has a problem he wants to solve *right now.*

What Do You Offer?

You said to the referral: "I have to discover if you need what I have to offer." In order to move forward you must be very clear about exactly what you offer. This is much more than a list of products. It's a process whereby you discover whether the benefits that are associated with the products you offer are benefits the suspect actually want to investigate at this time. Developing a simple questionnaire will help you uncover your client's needs.

How to Determine What You Offer

Here's your assignment. Sit down with a piece of paper and draw a line right down the middle from top to bottom. On the left side list the benefits that your products and services provide to your clients. On the right side list the corresponding questions you need to ask to determine if the suspect needs these benefits now.

A benefit is the outcome the buyer experiences having bought and used your products or services. You could call the benefit: "the product of my product." The questions that you list on the right side of the questionnaire ask: Do you need the benefits that I provide? Do you want to solve your problems now?

Sample Q & A – Initial Interview Questionnaire

BENEFITS YOU PROVIDE	QUESTIONS YOU CAN ASK
Adequate Retirement Income	On a scale of 1-6 (with 6 being highest), how secure do you feel about your retirement program?
Good Feeling about College Education Funding	On a scale of 1-6, how well do you think your college funding program is working?
Passing Desired Amounts of Assets to Your Children	How well does your current estate plan allocate the amount of assets that will pass to your children?
Business Continuity	On a scale of 1-6, what is your degree of satisfaction that your business will continue to do well, even after you've moved on?

Assume that you sell life insurance. Your *specific product* is a life insurance contract. The *product of your product* is the benefit your buyer feels, such as: "I have a sense of financial security; peace of mind; a sense of satisfaction that I am caring for my family. I feel good about the way I am providing for the continuation of my business. I am happy I can send my child to college. I feel good knowing my children will be well cared for even if I am not around."

Thus the "product of my product" (the benefit or value proposition) is the feeling the person gets as a result of actually acquiring the specific product or service you provide. When you list the benefits your products or services provide, you may come up with six, eight, or ten different value propositions your products offer. You have to look at each product or service and ask, "How does the person feel as a result of buying this product or service?"

If, for example, the benefit of buying a life insurance policy is financial security and peace of mind, then the question you could ask would be, "How comfortable are you that your family would be properly cared for in the event of your premature death?" Another question: "How satisfied are you that your education plan will work if you die prematurely?" "Do you have a plan that guarantees your children can finish college even if you're no longer around to support them?" Another question: "Do you have a high degree of confidence that your family would be able to maintain its current standard of living if you died prematurely?"

Key point: you can only truly know the benefits you provide by asking your clients to describe the values and benefits they've received by dealing with you. You determine whether your prospects want the benefits you provide by asking your clients penetrating questions. Thus, you would probably not ask, "Do you want more life insurance?" The reason is they may not know whether they want more life insurance. They may not know whether they need more life insurance. That is why we will ask feeling questions in the opening interview and throughout the sales process.

Developing Your Initial Interview Questionnaire

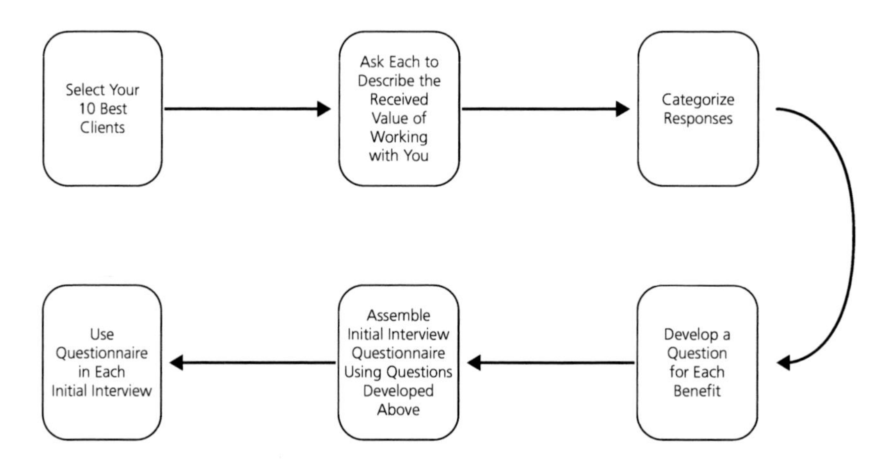

Based on the concept of discovery-then-persuasion, the initial interviews questionnaire is designed to help you discover three important facts:

1. Is the chemistry good between you and the prospect?
2. Does this prospect want to deal with *you*?
3. Is your prospect motivated to move forward at this time?

Your 15-20 minute meeting will provide you enough time to have your suspect answer these three questions (by completing the initial interview questionnaire) and have a conversation with you.

How to Discover the Values You Offer – The Value Proposition

Select your ten best clients and ask them to describe the value they have received by working with you. You need to know how your client would describe the "product of your product" – or the benefits they received. Peter Drucker summed this up nicely:

> The final question needed in order to come to grips with the business purpose and mission is: "What is value to the customer?" It may be the most important question. Yet it is the one least often asked. One reason is that managers are quite sure they know the answer. Value is what they, in their business, define as quality. But this is almost always the wrong definition. The customer never buys a product. By definition the customer buys the satisfaction of a want. He buys value....What a company's different customers consider value is so complicated that it can be answered only by the customers themselves. Management should not even try to guess at the answers – it should always go to the customers in a systematic quest for them.
>
> – From *The Daily Drucker*

Drucker, *The Daily Drucker: 366 Days of Insight and Motivation for Getting the Right Things Done*, 64.

How To Use the "Value" Responses

The responses you receive will tell you what your clients appreciate about working with you. You want this feedback because it tells you exactly how to discover if your suspect is actually a prospect for your products and services. Follow this simple process:

Using the flow chart on page 70 and the format of the sample below, develop an 8-10 question initial interview questionnaire.

Sample Initial Interview Questionnaire

YOUR PRODUCT	RESPONSES YOU'VE RECEIVED (CLIENT VALUES)	QUESTIONS YOU ASK (ALL QUESTIONS CAN BE ANSWERED ON A SCALE OF 1-6 WITH 6 HIGH)	I WANT TO SOLVE THIS PROBLEM NOW (1-6)
529 Plans	College Education Secured	How comfortable are you with your current college funding program?	
Life Insurance	Sense of security about financial affairs at date of death	How satisfied are you with the security your current life insurance program provides?	
Retirement Plans	Feel really good about overall retirement plan	How confident are you that your current retirement program is adequate?	
Long Term Care Insurance	I'm not a burden to my children if disabled	Do you have enough money to pay for two households?	
Will and Trust Planning	My heirs won't be fighting over my assets	How current is your estate plan?	

Investment Plan Asset Allocation	I'm very satisfied with my investment program	How comfortable are you with your current asset allocation?
Reports	It's really great to have all my assets listed in one report	Degree of satisfaction about simplicity and organization of investment reports?

Type the questionnaire and print it out on your letterhead or presentation sheet. Use this questionnaire anytime you need an efficient – and easy – method to help you qualify a suspect.

Initial Interview Agenda

You should also create an agenda for your interview. This will help you stay focused and keep on track during the little time you have. Here's an example:

Agenda Prepared for: Jess Kennedy-Williams
Date: November 20, 2009

Item 1	Do you have any questions about the products or services I provide?
Item 2	Do you have questions about my background experience or credentials?
Item 3	Complete the Initial Interview Questionnaire
Item 4	Evaluate Initial Interview Questionnaire answers
Item 5	What's our next step?

Typed on your letterhead.

Arriving Mentally Prepared for the Interview

When you go into this appointment it's important to be very well organized and know the specific objectives of the interview.

1. Know the basic objectives of the interview:
   - Evaluate chemistry
   - Discover if the suspect is a prospect
   - Discover if the suspect is a prospect for your products / services now
2. Bring a written agenda.
3. Bring the initial interview questionnaire.
4. Bring a copy of your printed fact finder. Just in case...
5. Put items 2-4 into your standard file, and make sure the subject's name is on the file, preferably typed.

I suggest having a printed fact finder on hand because you may, from time to time, meet with a person who wants to move forward right away. It's important to be prepared. We haven't talked much about fact finders, but we will in the next chapter. Being organized means that you've planned ahead and that you're always prepared to move to the next step in the sales process.

By presenting the agenda and an initial interview questionnaire, you'll be able to complete the initial interview in your 15-20 minute time allotment. Being prepared means you'll be able to honor the agreement made when the initial interview appointment was set.

At the end of the interview, provide a recap. It could go like this: "Jess, based upon the answers to this questionnaire, and the sense that I have that we could work well together, our next step is to meet again for a more comprehensive interview. At that appointment I'll be able to get more detailed and thorough information about your particular wants and needs. Is this something you'd like to do?"

Stop and listen for the answer. If your assessment of the situation is correct, you've converted a suspect to a prospect who wants to use you and your services now...and you did this in about 15-20 minutes. Set up the next appointment *now*.

Fuzzy Answers – Do You Have a Prospect?

If you get a fuzzy answer or objections, you must deal with the concerns being expressed. Perhaps the suspect has another agent, or perhaps your timing is not right. Whatever the objection or hesitation, there are only three possible outcomes.

Outcome 1 – No-for-Now

It may be that you can overcome the objection or hesitation and deal with it effectively enough to continue. The No-For-Now response has been converted to a Yes.

Outcome 2 – No-for-Now or No-Forever?

The decision to move forward is inappropriate at this time, but it may be possible at some future time (this is also a no-for-now answer). Add this person to your prospect list.

Outcome 3 – No-Forever

You determine that the chemistry is not right, or the need is not there, or that the timing will never be right. This answer is *no forever*; you should be prepared with a gracious exit.

Here's something you might say: "Jess, I've enjoyed talking with you this morning and it doesn't appear that there's a good fit between my services and your needs. I want to thank you for the time we spent together. Let me give you my card, and if ever you should change your mind please give me a call. I'd be happy to work with you when it's good timing for you."

Or you may say: "Jess, it doesn't appear that the timing is right for us at this point, and you don't need my services at this time. Thanks for your time. Please feel free to call me if I can be of help to you."

Opening Interview Evaluation

Let's recap what you and your suspect talked about in this opening interview.

- Did you present the agenda?
- Was there good chemistry?

- Was the initial interview questionnaire completed?
- If the suspect was a prospect, did he / she agree to set up a date for the next meeting?
- If not a good prospect, did you have a graceful exit?

Regardless of the sales outcome of the interview, the goal is to always handle yourself professionally and efficiently by having all the interview pieces lined up prior to the initial interview.

In Chapter Seven we'll discuss completing the fact finder. Because the fact finding interview, or information gathering interview, is the most important part of the sales process, it takes the most time. A completed, printed fact finder provides you with the most important sales information (what's important to your prospect), and provides an easy method to obtain the basic information to successfully complete the three other marketing opportunities (who's important, COI information and demo – and psychographic information).

Opening the Case Highlights

- ❖ Develop standard language for setting an initial interview.
- ❖ Be clear about your objectives for the appointment.
- ❖ Ask your best clients to tell you the benefits they received from using your products and services (value propositions).
- ❖ Develop an initial interview questionnaire to discover if you have a prospect who wants to solve his financial planning problems now.
- ❖ Learn how to deal with objections to seeing you, but only try to overcome objections once or twice.
- ❖ Never leave an appointment without a clear commitment to taking the next step – or close the case.
- ❖ Learn how to differentiate between no-for-now and no forever.
- ❖ Have all your initial interview requirements in your suspect's opening the case file.

SIX

Mental Gymnastics

When Setting the Initial Interview

You will get objections: it's to be expected almost any place in the sales process. A basic attitude I use throughout this book is that we are not trying to overpower or overwhelm a prospective client either to set an appointment or take our recommendations. We want to deal with objections or questions as they arise, and to take "no" if that is the right answer. There are usually two basic objections to meeting with you:

1. The suspect knows what you do and does not want or need your services.
2. The suspect does not know what you do, but is still unsure about meeting with you.

Whatever the objection, you should be prepared to deal with it – at least once, twice at most. You could say, "Ms. Suspect, if I hear you correctly you are not certain at this time that you need the services that I offer. Is that right?" Typically the answer is yes.

You then say, "Well, I can understand that, but the only way we'll truly know if I can be of help to you is if we meet for a brief period of time, and I promise that at the end of the fifteen or twenty minutes we'll both know if you need my services. If the answer is no, I will thank you for your time and be on my way. So, with that thought in mind could we meet?" and you see if you can set the appointment.

Another common objection is, "Well, I have another advisor. I don't think I need your services." This may be a legitimate objection or not. You could respond by saying, "I understand that you have been dealing with someone else. In fact, Ellen mentioned that you might have another advisor. But she was so impressed with what I was able to do for her that she said, 'Please tell Jess that even if she is working with someone else it would certainly make sense for her to check you out because it might be to her advantage to see you.' So, with that thought in mind I'm wondering, again, if we might meet next week on Tuesday or Wednesday at the requested time."

I believe you should *NOT* typically try to overcome objections more than once. Twice is the absolute maximum. You are looking for someone who *already* wants to solve their financial problems. If you don't receive a positive response, it's probably not a good fit – at least not at this time. If you receive a lot of no's to your initial call, then you should evaluate your prospecting process and what kinds of prospects you're looking for. (You should get about 5 appointments for every 10 referrals you reach.)

Three Helpful Sales Attitudes

There are three attitudes to foster to help your sales activities. First, hold a discovery mindset. Second, be willing to deal with "No." Third, realize the sales process only moves forward with affirmative responses at each step of the process.

Attitude 1: Discovery – Then Persuasion

Your first basic objective should be to *discover* whether or not a person needs your services – persuasion comes later. By having a discovery mindset, any business between you and your prospect will be a win for both of you, as it will be based on the client's true needs. On the other hand, if you benefit by making a sale, but the buyer doesn't feel satisfied – that's not a good relationship because it's not a win for both parties. Solve the client's problem, and you will be on your way to achieving your long-term financial objectives.

The attitude of *win-win* is fundamental and critical in the entire sales process. I cannot stress too strongly how much trouble you get into when your only intention or objective is to make a sale with little regard for the client's wishes. You lose customers, you fail to build a sustainable client base, and you end up with more stress and worry than you'd like.

Attitude 2: What Part of "No" Don't You Understand?

The *next* attitude that needs to be included in your mindset is the willingness to *deal with "No."* It's critical that you deal with prospect / client objections in an open and forthright manner. No matter how powerful a salesperson you are, no matter how persuasive you are, failure to deal with the concept of "No" in an effective, honest and forthright manner will hurt your sales success in the long run.

It doesn't necessarily mean you have to spend a lot of time dealing with an objection; it may be a simple objection, such as, "Oh I thought my only choice was to pay an annual premium." I say, "Oh no. You have several choices: you can pay on a monthly, quarterly or a semiannual basis as well."

When you are presented with a more complex objection, it is imperative you deal honestly with the concern. As we mentioned in Chapter Three, there are three possible responses to any question where you ask your client to take action. It's your job to classify the answer correctly.

Number one: "*Yes*, I will move forward. I will do what you want me to do" or "I will do what is necessary to do."

Number two: "No, I will not do what you want. I will not move forward" in which case the case is dead. That's "no forever." The sales process is over and you should exit gracefully.

Number three: "No-for-now," which simply means that the prospect can't make a decision at this time, but might be able to see you at a later date. "No-for-now" could also be a temporary interruption caused by a simple misunderstanding. Whichever variation, this case is still alive. No-for-now is a legitimate objection.

It's the inability to effectively deal with "no" that prolongs the sales process and wastes so much time and leaves you with the belief you have a prospect when you don't.

Attitude 3: Keep the Sales Process Moving

See "The Sales Process" chart on page 64.

It's critically important to understand where you are in the sales process. There may be six, eight, ten, or twelve steps that need to be completed before the sale is made. Unless you receive an affirmative response at the end of each sales step, you should not assume the sale is moving forward. An example: When you called the referral to set an initial interview appointment, you needed to receive an affirmative response to meet with you, or the sales process was dead. This is an unbreakable requirement, inherent in every single step of the sales process. You *must* ask for, and receive an affirmative response to each step to keep the process moving forward.

Some Examples

STEP	OBJECTIVE	REQUIREMENT	REMINDER
Contact the Referral	Set the initial interview appointment	Get agreement to meet at a specific time and place	Always have a specific date for the next step
Set the opening interview time	Determine if you have a prospect	Complete an initial interview questionnaire	Do not move forward unless suspect completes initial interview questionnaire

STEP	OBJECTIVE	REQUIREMENT	REMINDER
Conduct the fact finder interview	Gather all relevant facts and feelings	Determine if needs exist and it's a compelling issue	Always set agreement to go to the next step – no matter how small a step
Talk to members of the buying committee	Contact members of buying committee to get accurate picture of all needs and objections	Gain permission to contact key advisors	You must have a good reason to talk to all buying committee members
Set up the closing interview	Make the sale	Have a simple closing presentation	A good close should be simple – because you've done all your homework prior to the close

An Obvious – But Not so Obvious – Roadblock

Occasionally, we get a response that looks good – but isn't. I call this response "the kiss of death." Many years ago, the response to my presentation was, "Gee Nick, that's the best presentation I've ever seen. It's exactly what I wanted to see. Thank you so much." The praise was effusive, and while at the time it struck me as being a little bit odd (because people don't normally react that way), I still thought the process was moving forward. It wasn't. The effusive praise was just a way to avoid moving to the next step in the sales process. I could never get a commitment to move to the next step.

Unfortunately, I did not make the sale. The praise was simply a way of disarming me so that the prospect could say no, without saying no directly. It was actually confusing. I thought, "If this is such a great presentation, why aren't you agreeing to move to the next step?" I didn't initially put two-and-two together. But of course the intention of this prospect was to confuse the issue so that he didn't have to move forward.

Another possibility was that I was pushing too hard, and made it very difficult for the prospect to express his true wishes. One of the effects of not truly hearing your prospect is that *your* lack of sensitivity actually encourages your client to lie to you. Even prospects who don't want to buy often have a hard time saying no – directly.

What would I do now? I would confront the issue this way: "Mr. Prospect, I am delighted that you think this presentation has done such a good job of identifying your issues. The next step is for us to begin to implement this program. How do you feel about that?"

The answer that you get immediately tells you whether or not you can continue the sales process. In this case the answer would have been, "Well, I'm not prepared to move forward at this time." Now you have an opportunity to deal with objections, discover the buyer's reluctance, and deal honestly with their basic issues. Who knows what is behind the reluctance? You'll never know unless you ask.

- It could be that he's got somebody else that he's dealing with.
- He might be embarrassed because he doesn't have the money to move forward.
- He may have changed his mind because what he thought he wanted is not what you presented.
- He may not know how to say "no" in a direct and forthright manner.

Whatever the basis for his objection or resistance, you must deal with the issues before you can go on to the next step. Do not delude yourself into thinking that you have a sale and can move forward.

What you need at each sales step: a "yes." Then you can move on. The next step may simply be returning a form. It may be providing you with a balance sheet, or taking a physical exam, or calling the attorney to set up a meeting. Whatever the requirement is, moving on to the next step can only occur if the requirement is satisfied. There is no way you can avoid this requirement and still make the sale.

Your Attitude Counts

A great deal of the tension in the sales process can be eliminated if your attitude is simply to discover what your client needs, deal with objections honestly and to only move forward only when appropriate.

SEVEN

Information Gathering

The only attitude that is truly productive and sustainable in the long run in sales is a win-win attitude. Essentially, this means that the transaction engaged in is good for both the buyer and the seller.

It's a win for the buyer if buying your products and services solves a problem and provides value. The only way to uncover the prospect's problems or needs is to ask specific questions. In the information gathering phase of the sale's process, your most effective approach is discovery first, then persuasion.

A good discovery process is the key to successful selling while maintaining a win-win attitude. The discovery process is based upon using a printed fact finder.

Take the following assessment to evaluate your present discovery process.

Fact Finder Assessment

Do you use a fact finder on a regular basis?

____

Is it a printed fact finder?

____

Does it ask fact questions about each area in which you can provide solutions to client problems?

____

Does it ask feeling questions about _each_ area in which you can provide solutions to client problems?

____

Does it capture the names of future prospects (client referrals)?

Does it capture the names of potential referrals to other professionals (COI referrals)?

Does it capture the important psychographic and demographic information about your clients? (This information can help refine your target market profile.)

Does it capture all of the important compliance information that either your broker / dealer or the insurance company that you work with requires in order to meet compliance requirements?

Does your fact finder ask background questions about each benefit area you serve?

After taking this assessment, you may find you do not have or use a printed fact finder. The importance of a fact finder cannot be overstated. In my opinion, it is the *most important tool* in the most crucial part of the sales process. If you don't use it to its fullest extent, you are missing incredible sales and marketing opportunities.

Using a Fact Finder – An Example

Imagine that you are a medical doctor and a surgeon. A patient comes into your office and after you greet the patient, you say: "Mr. Patient. I'm so glad you came in today. You know, I'm having a sale on appendectomies and I think you could really benefit by having an appendectomy performed within two weeks. Even if you don't have a problem right now, it will save you trouble in the future. You will never have to worry about appendicitis. And as an added incentive my normal fee of $5000 is going to be reduced to $3,500. Can we schedule you for surgery in about ten days or two weeks?"

This example is intentionally absurd. No doctor or professional person of any kind functions this way. The reason is simple. No professional ever proposes a solution until they discover the problem. That professional standard should apply to financial advisors as well. Never present a solution until the problem is uncovered and there is agreement between you and the prospect that a problem truly exists.

How do you do that? Simple: regularly use a fact finder or information gathering form. In dealing with hundreds of agents, I haven't found that many agents use a printed fact finder. The end result is that these advisors are not nearly as effective as they could be, because they don't get the information listed below.

What Your Fact Finder Will Help You Accomplish

Your fact finder should help you accomplish four basic tasks:

#1 – DISCOVER THE PROSPECT'S FINANCIAL NEEDS AND CONCERNS

It helps you discover the prospect's financial needs and concerns. Being thorough at this stage establishes your competence, allows the prospect to trust you, and provides a pathway to being able to recommend appropriate solutions to the client's wants and needs. *(What's important?)*

#2 – DISCOVER WHO IS IMPORTANT TO YOUR PROSPECT

A good fact finder can also help you discover *who* is important in your prospect's business and personal life. Who are the people that your client would turn to in the event of a financial or emotional crisis? These are the people who are important to your client; and they very well could be people you'd like to talk to in the future. By capturing these names while gathering basic financial and personal information, you will be able to feed these names to your client when having a referral conversation at some future time. *(Who's important?)*

#3 – DISCOVER THE QUALITY OF YOUR PROSPECT'S PROFESSIONAL RELATIONSHIPS

The third marketing opportunity lies in discovering the quality of your client's professional relationships. Is the client happy with his mortgage broker? Is the client happy with his doctor, his attorney, or his accountant? If the prospect or client is less than totally satisfied (satisfied is a 5 or 6 on a scale of 1 to 6), this may present you with an opportunity to recommend other professionals to your client. These professionals may, in turn, refer prospects back to you *(COI information)*.

Inquiry about the quality of professional relationships has two advantages. First, it may help your client run his or her business affairs more effectively with better advisors. Second, it provides you with an opportunity to develop a professional relationship that could result in reciprocal referrals. This will not happen, however, unless you inquire and discover how satisfactory the relationships are that your prospect or client has with his advisors.

#4 – PSYCHOGRAPHIC AND DEMOGRAPHIC CHARACTERISTICS

The fourth element to be discovered from the use of a fact finder is the capture of important psychographic and demographic characteristics of your clients / prospects.

These characteristics – psychological, financial and personal – can be used to help you develop a better profile of your target market. You gain three advantages when you are able to more accurately define your target market:

1. You can be more specific and descriptive when seeking client referrals
2. You'll be able to better manage your Center of Influence referral system
3. You'll have a solid basis for setting up a Center of Service referral network system

These data can also be used to help you identify your ideal clients within your target market. As stated earlier, you don't choose your target market or your ideal client. Your target market and ideal client choose you *(target market information)*.

Why Feelings Are Important

I have collected more than twenty fact finders from various financial institutions. They generally do a good job of capturing facts and figures, assets, liabilities, home addresses, family members, and often, a balance sheet. But most fact finders do not do nearly as good of a job of gathering information about the feelings and concerns your clients have about their financial and business affairs. A challenge to you: do you use a printed fact finder that enables you to satisfy the four fact finder criteria listed above?

Ron Willingham, author of *Integrity Selling For The Twenty-First Century,* asserts that 85% of the selling process has to do with feelings, and only 15% has to do with facts and product knowledge. The fact finder is the perfect tool to help you discover more of the 85%, that part which pertains to feelings. What matters to your client? What's important? In fact, the best question you can ask is: "What's important to you?" The answer will be revealing.

How Do I Find One of These Fact Finders?

Here are some sources for fact finders:

1. Ask your company for a fact finder.
2. Ask some of the vendors whose products you sell if they have a fact finder.
3. Design your own fact finder.
4. Open *Toolsformoney.com* and review their collection of fact finders. *Toolsformoney* has the best collection of fact finders I've seen, and their fact finders are designed for people in the financial services industry. Their fact finders are Word documents, and can be easily modified to meet your specific selling requirements and compliance standards.

When you have generated a printed fact finder, you need to ask:

- Does it provide you with information to complete your CRM (Customer Relationship Management) software input requirements?
- Does your fact finder capture all the information needed to generate a proposal for the software proposal system you use?
- Does it capture enough information to complete a financial planning proposal?
- Does your fact finder capture all necessary information to meet your company or broker dealer compliance requirements?

How to Design a Fact Finder

Your fact finder should ask questions which reflect the benefits that you provide so that you can offer advice and solutions for your client's needs. You can determine how quickly your client wants to move and can gather useful marketing information at the same time.

A Section for Each Service You Offer

A fact finder should ask questions which are based on the benefits that you provide. As an example, look at the questions you asked in the initial interview questionnaire. Those questions allowed your prospects to determine if they needed the benefits that you provide.

Your fact finder must have a section for each area in which you provide expert advice and effective solutions to client problems. You should follow this questioning process whether your service is simple or complex.

Here's a simple example: let's say that you sell gardening shovels, typically found in hardware stores. You sell lightweight shovels, with ergonomic handles –especially good for people who garden and sometimes get sore backs in the process. Some questions might be: Do you do any gardening? Are you happy with your current shovel? Do you have any back problems when you garden? Even a fact finder about a product as simple as a shovel could actually prove to be fairly complex.

ADD A BUYING COMMITTEE SECTION

Your fact finder should have a section we can call "The Buying Committee." Any time there is more than one person making – or influencing – the buying decision, a political aspect is added to the equation. You should contact each of these people. Failure to do so could lead to big surprises at the closing interview. I'm sure you'd agree you should discover who is on your client or prospect's buying committee – and make sure you have included their input in your closing presentation.

OFFER EXPERT ADVICE AND EFFECTIVE SOLUTIONS

Imagine that you sell disability income insurance. Simply asking if a person has disability income insurance is the beginning of this investigational process. We know that one of the benefits of owning disability income insurance is that you, as the policy owner, can say that you have the peace of mind of knowing that your income will continue even if you are unable to work and earn a living. You could continue your inquiry by saying, "Tell me about your disability program." Then you could ask how the person feels about his current program or his existing coverage.

Dig deep to discover how your prospect feels about the issue of continuing income in the event of a disability. You might ask the prospect if she feels she has enough assets to carry her through. And even if she has enough assets to cover a lengthy disability, does she want to deplete her assets this way?

Your deep understanding of disability income insurance will enable you to ask pertinent questions pertaining to your prospect's concerns. The answers will guide you to make appropriate recommendations. Unless you have a clear picture of how the loss of earnings can impact a family; unless you've actually seen it; unless you've gone through the claims process, you cannot truly offer your client good advice and make appropriate recommendations.

A fact finder allows you to easily record your prospect's answers to these questions regarding disability income insurance. This give and take conversation will allow you to ultimately make appropriate disability income policy and planning recommendations.

Discover the Nature and Depth of the Problem

In collaborative or consultative selling, it is the advisor's job to discover the true problem – from the buyer's point of view. We may believe that we truly understand the buyer's problem, and that our products and services are perfectly suited to solve *our* perception of the problem. This attitude misses the crucial role we have when completing a fact finder: to discover the answer to these issues from the *buyer's* point of view.

What does the buyer believe the critical issue to be? Ask the buyer these questions:

See "The Sales Process" chart on page 64 to better understand how these critical questions fit into the overall sales process.

- What is the central issue from your point of view?
- What is the result if you don't solve this problem now?
- On a scale of 1-6 how important is it to solve your problem now?
- Do you have funds allocated to solve this problem now, if we provide a solution to it?
- Are you willing to move forward with me now to investigate how we can help you solve your problem?

How Quickly Does Your Client Want to Move?

Use the questions in your initial interview questionnaire as a template for the type of questions used in your complete fact finder. Every product and every service you provide should trigger appropriate questions for you to ask. The reason: You should not make a product or service recommendation until you are sure your prospect has a problem he wants to solve. And you can't know if a person has a problem he wants to solve unless you ask him about it.

We're not saying you necessarily should ask, "Do you have a problem with your disability income program?" or "Do you want to buy more disability income insurance?" Rather, we'd ask, "What would happen if you became disabled?" "What would you want to happen from an economic point of view?" The questions make sense if you, as the advisor, have a program that would provide a solution to this problem. The fundamental equation we use throughout the entire selling process is, "Do you have a problem for which we have a solution?"

If and when you discover that your prospect has a problem, you then want to know how quickly the prospect wants to solve the problem. Let's continue using the disability income insurance example. If you reach the point where the prospect says, "I don't have enough disability income insurance and it would be a problem if I were to become disabled," one might assume, "I've got a sale! My prospect wants to buy more disability income insurance." Be careful – the mere fact that a person expresses concern doesn't automatically mean that there is concern enough to buy a policy now. You should use his positive response to reinforce the sale when you return to make your presentation and close.

AN EXAMPLE

Let us assume that you have discovered that your prospect does not have a good disability income program, and you believe your prospect should buy $5,000 a month of additional disability income insurance protection. What does the prospect think? Ask him!

You might say, "Mr. Prospect, we've discovered it would be a problem if you became disabled and lost your income. As you currently have no disability income insurance other than state and federal benefits, you have a big gap in your program." Now ask this critical question: "On a scale of 1-6, with 6 being highest, how serious a problem is this from your point of view?" If it's a six, then ask, "On a scale of 1-6, how willing are you to commit your funds to solve this problem now?"

In order to make a sale, you have to determine if the buyer is concerned. And you also have to determine if the buyer feels the urgency to solve this problem *now*. This example demonstrates that persuasiveness is not as critical as discovery. Action is only taken when the buyer reveals that he has a problem and is not satisfied maintaining the status quo.

All your persuasive power in the world won't mean much if the buyer doesn't feel the urgency. You may be very persuasive and effective in moving your prospect from a neutral position to a positive position. But you must also find out if your prospect feels the need for the product and is willing to spend money to buy it *now*.

The fact finder has all of these important issues built in, which is why the fact finder is the most critical step in the sales process. Important facts such as family members, place of employment, current earnings, social security number, or balance sheet are all data that a person could provide to you without your involvement. But you have a crucially important responsibility to discover what's important to your clients, how urgently they feel the need to solve their problems *now*.

See a sample Fact Finder in Appendix 1 on page 139.

The Fact Finder as a Marketing Tool

In addition to helping you discover how quickly the client wants to solve his financial problems, the fact finder also provides you with valuable marketing information. Names of future referrals and valuable referrals you can give to other professionals are revealed with the help of your fact finder. The fact finder also serves as a data collection form for helping you discover the important psychographic and demographic characteristics of your client or prospect.

I guarantee that if you use a printed, well thought out fact finder you will become more efficient, more effective and more profitable. You will also avoid any compliance issues and make it easier to enter CRM client information data and proposal information in an efficient manner.

Print It Out

Your marketing efforts generated referrals; contacting the referrals was the first step in the sales process, followed by the initial interview, which is followed by the information gathering stage where you made extensive use of the fact finder.

I have observed that many sales professionals dislike paperwork, forms, record keeping, etc. That is why so many representatives consider a yellow pad (legal or letter size) to be the ideal data gathering form.

I challenge that assumption – I believe failure to use a printed fact finder robs you of a multitude of benefits.

If we compress all the attitudes, ideas and sales suggestions made so far, here is how the well-designed, printed fact finder can serve your clients and also aid your marketing efforts.

Sales Process Key Points: Effective Mental Preparation

- Hold an attitude of discovery, then persuasion.
- Base your transactions on a win-win proposition.
- Always be prepared to hear and deal with "no."
- Base your sales process on helping the client *first*;
  a true professional is committed to doing what's right,
  and not just making the sale.
- Remember to demand an affirmative response to each step in the sales process. You can create a reminder to ask for a yes to each step on your printed fact finder.

Adeptly Manage the Information Gathering Interview

You must have a clear picture of the products and services you provide. During your fact finding process, you can gather information and uncover attitudes your prospect has about your products and services. Ask follow-up questions when a hidden agenda issue, an objection, or any other piece of important information is uncovered or revealed. By being thorough, you will truly discover what is important to your prospect and become more adept at managing the fact finding interview.

Fact Finder Highlights

- A printed fact finder will help you capture the names of future prospects.
- Your fact finder will help you gather the names of your prospect's professional relationships –and the level of satisfaction your prospect has with each of these people.
- Your fact finder can also help you gather psychographic and demographic information about your client or prospect. This data can be used to discover your true target market profile (you know – the ones who choose you).
- Studies have shown that a simple checklist is a very effective tool for staying on track and covering all the important points of *any* process. A printed fact finder is such a checklist: it keeps you on track and helps you gather all the information you need to make appropriate product and service recommendations to your prospect or client.
- A printed fact finder can – and should – be designed to gather all the information you need to populate your CRM software and proposal software input fields.
- Your fact finder can also help you meet your company or broker / dealer compliance requirements.
- A printed fact finder conveys a professional skill set.
- Your printed fact finder will remind you to discover the political aspects of the buying decision, by discovering all the members of the buying committee.

EIGHT

Closing the Case

Let's follow the steps you've completed in the sales process thus far and "close the case." First, you obtained permission to see the suspect. In your opening interview, you determined if you had a prospect who wanted to move forward – now. Next, you completed a printed fact finder, talked to the members of the buying committee, and prepared a presentation that recaps the prospect's problems and your solutions to these problems.

Your next step: Closing the case, where you present your findings and ask for the order. If you clearly understand the client's needs, it is normal to think you have a perfect solution, and that a sale is imminent.

Yet, we often find that the sale is not made. Industry averages show that only about 1 out of every 3 closes results in a sale. A case typically gets derailed for one or two fundamental reasons. Number one, it fails to close because there was insufficient discussion with the other people who had some influence on the buying decision. The other members of the buying committee had issues or concerns that were not addressed in your presentation. Thus, no sale! Number two, you probably did not discover enough information about the buyer's wants and desires. And sometimes when you have better information, you may even discover that you did not have a good prospect, and you should not have presented your proposal or wasted your time on a futile effort.

Closing the Case Assessment

What You Can Do to Improve Your Closing Ratio

I complete a printed fact finder.

I identify all members of the "buying committee."

I speak with each member of the "buying committee."

If possible, I have an inside contact to help guide me through a complex sale.

I discover my prospect's most important goals and concerns, and how important it is to solve these problems now.

I discover and deal with all objections prior to the closing interview.

The closing interview is scheduled and interruption-free.

See more about buying styles on p 102.

My presentation format matches my prospect's buying style.

I use a brief presentation summary as the basis for my closing interview.

I have a case file with requirements listed for issuing the case.

All necessary forms are completed (to the extent possible) prior to the closing interview.

I discuss all health and financial requirements to have the case issued (including possible problems).

I discuss all other requirements for case issuance and have a completion date for each one.

I describe my case delivery procedures.

I inquire about any questions or concerns regarding case issuance.

I describe my underwriting follow-up procedures to assure that the case is issued in a timely fashion.

The Political Side of Making a Sale – "The Buying Committee"

This is often the elephant in the room, obvious but not dealt with. Not only do you need to know about the client's clearly stated needs, you should also know all of the people who have an influence on the buying decision. Many times the members of the "buying committee" are not readily identified. Clues come when you hear: "Well I like it, but I have to run this by my accountant...my attorney...my business advisor... my friend...my wife...the other salesman I've dealt with for twenty-two years...whomever." All of these people may have some influence on the decision and can certainly derail the case.

When others (in addition to the obvious buyer) influence the buying decision, you have a complex sale. A complex sale does not necessarily refer to a complex product; sometimes it refers to a complex buying- or decision-making process. Thus, any sale is a complex sale when more than one person influences the final buying decision.

When the sale is complex, your job is to inquire about the prospect's buying decision process. For example: You're working with a buyer who is selecting financial services for his company; you and he are getting along well; the rapport is excellent, and the information you have gathered about his needs and concerns is well defined. At this point you may be lulled into thinking that you've got the sale. What if this case is a complex sale?

On further investigation, you discover that there are many people who influence the final buying decision. Your job is to discover how to reach and talk to all members on the "buying committee" – those who have an impact and can either derail or ensure that the sale is made. This often happens regardless of the quality of your relationship with the nominal buyer.

How to Deal with the Buying Committee

In some cases, the buying committee members are known. In other cases, you suspect there is a committee but don't know its members. If this is so, you might say something like, "Ms. Prospect, if I were in your situation I would be talking to other important people in the company before I made a final buying decision. I suspect that's your situation as well. Who else is on your buying committee? Who else will have an impact on your ultimate decision? Now I realize that you're the main decision maker, but I also suspect others will have an impact. So who's on your buying committee that I should talk to?"

Wait for the answer. It may be somebody who is not at all obvious to you. It might be that your prospect has a mentor in the company whom she'll talk with who is not even in the chain of command. She may have a friend with whom she'd consult. You can see why it's your job is to ask the question, "Who's on your buying committee?" Any one of these people may have some impact or influence on the ultimate buying decision.

Having discovered the identity of these previously invisible people, it is now your responsibility to talk to them. Any one of them, even those with only minor input, can raise an issue that you're unaware of, or that even your prospect is unaware of. Failure to address these hidden or underground issues may have a significant impact on successfully making the sale.

I can't tell you how many times I've heard financial advisors say, "I hate CPAs. They just mess up my cases." Or how many times I have gotten an objection that seemed to come out of left field. If you are ever surprised in the closing interview, it usually is because *you failed to get the necessary information in the fact finding interview.*

Dealing with Objections to Meeting Buying Committee Members

If your prospect is reluctant to introduce you to other members of the buying committee, it is important that you deal directly with this issue. Make it clear that these meetings will be in your prospect's best interest.

An Imaginary Conversation

"Ms. Prospect, I know that I will likely have only one opportunity to present my case to you – to truly solve your problems. I'm interested in making sure that my presentation presents solutions to your problems.

I'm also interested in making a presentation to the members of your buying committee that will effectively deal with all of their needs and concerns as well. If there's any information or expectation that impacts the ultimate buying decision and neither of us knows about it, at the very least we'll provide an incomplete proposal. And it may be that both of us end up looking like we didn't do our job as well as we should have. That is why I need to talk to all the players involved.

Anybody who's involved in the buying decision should be contacted. An objection might be, "Well, you know, my accountant charges $500 an hour." If it's an important enough case, say, "I understand. I am perfectly willing to pay for your accountant's time; I think this conversation is essential."

Anytime you get resistance about talking to the other members of the formal or informal buying committee, you may be walking into quicksand from which you cannot extricate yourself. Sometimes, by forcing this issue, you will discover that you're not in a very good selling position; that you're simply being used as a means to keep the competition honest. This is not an uncommon situation, but it's far better to know this *before* you've gone to all the work of putting your presentation together. On the other hand, pushing this issue may get you what you want: the interviews with committee members.

How frustrating is it if you discover that your buyer was only trying to please her boss, or trying to please herself that she was getting the best deal from her current vendor. You may have been asked for a proposal simply because you happened to be the perfect person at the time. This is a vexing situation and rarely leads to a sale. If you discover that you have little chance for a sale, you can make the decision to stop your sales activities before you invest any more time or money in what will usually end up as a fruitless effort.

Finding an Inside Contact

It can be very helpful to have a contact inside the organization who can act as a coach or supporter for you. This is a person who may not be on the buying committee, but who knows the players, the dynamics of the company and understands the corporate culture. Pray that you have a person like this available to you as it can be very, very helpful. Whether you have an inside contact or not, I can't overemphasize the need to talk to all the buying committee members to avoid being blindsided in the closing interview. Buyers often have many reasons to talk to you; many of these reasons do not include giving you an order.

Putting Together a Proposal

After having clear input from the buyer, and having dealt with all objections of the buying committee and the buyer, you can now prepare a proposal. The typical proposal starts with all of the details of the product and the company and then presents the solution and the price. I'm going to suggest that this is exactly backwards. I believe that the best way to present a case is to show the assumptions used in making your presentation and to then provide a summary and recommendations for solving your client's needs and problems.

Your formal presentation can be divided into two parts. Part One should only be two pages: 1) a recap of all the assumptions that are the basis for your recommendations; and 2) the recommendations that you are making to your client or prospect – and the call to action.

Part Two has all your supporting documentation. You need not review all of the facts when you get to the closing presentation. If you've done your homework and understand your client's or prospect's needs well, and have talked to the prospect and all the members of the buying committee, all you need is five or ten minutes to present your underlying assumptions and your recommendations.

In my opinion, hour- and two-hour closing presentations are too long. When you understand your client, his buying style, and his needs and desires, the close ought to be a low-keyed meeting. The hard and critically important steps have already been done in the fact finding and buying committee stages.

A Sample Closing Presentation

Exeter Manufacturing Corporation
401K Retirement Plan Summary

YOUR KEY ISSUES AND CONCERNS

1. Poor employee participation – currently fewer than 40% of all eligible employees invest in their 401K Plan.
2. Limited investment choices – only 4.
3. Infrequent benefit statements – now provided on a semi-annual basis only.
4. Excessive plan expenses for both assets charges and monthly fees – total current expenses exceed 3% of all plan investments. Currently is it $300,000 on plan assets of $10 million.
5. No regular and scheduled plan advisor meetings.
6. A too-long wait for plan sponsor return telephone calls. Return calls now take 2-3 business days.
7. Reduce response time for live calls.

OUR SOLUTIONS

1. We recommend an employee participation goal of 80% (based on buying committee input). Methods:
   - Web-based investment education programs
   - Semi-annual live investment training classes.
   - Change the company match formulas to $.50 / per dollar of each employee's contribution up to 6% of employee salary and bonuses.
   - Make enrollment automatic for each new employee. (Opt-out option.)
2. Increase investment choices to 18, including 6 lifestyle funds.
3. Provide monthly statements online and make them downloadable. Send printed annual statements by January 20th of each year.

4 Reduce total charges to 1.50% including asset charges and monthly fees and commissions. This will save the company and participants $150,000 per year.

5 Schedule two regular advisor meetings per year, with more as needed. We will also have a specific advisor assigned to your account.

6 Our telephone wait averages 45-60 seconds; your current vendor wait time is 6-8 minutes (based on 65 actual surveys).

A Strategic Presentation Approach

Another important consideration is to understand how your buyer wants information presented. According to Miller Heiman Incorporated, a well-known sales training organization, buyers fall into five categories:

1 Followers – 36%

2 Charismatics – 25%

3 Skeptics – 19%

4 Thinkers – 11%

5 Controllers – 9%

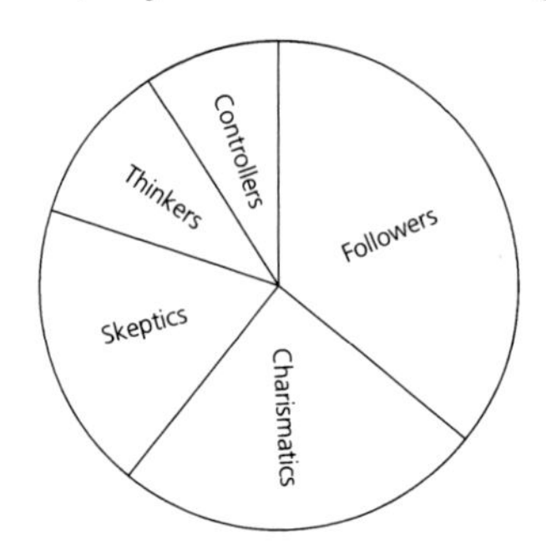

Miller, 11.

Each of these buyer categories has certain specific characteristics in terms of how they like to be sold. If you understand your prospect's buying style, it will allow you to present your case in the most effective and efficient manner.

Here's how this classification process works. Of the five types, the most common type is the Follower. The Follower, according to Miller Heiman, represents 36% of the buying public. If dealing with a Follower, these are the characteristics you'd look for:

- Do they seem to want confirmation or assurance that they're not the lone wolf, that they're not the first one out there?
- Has your prospect asked you who else has used your product?
- Are they very mindful of loss?

Your presentation to a Follower should be in this order:

1. Define the problem
2. Name and evaluate options
3. Describe why your option is best
4. Help assess the value of your option

Focus on what works now

It is very helpful to have your presentation style correspond to your prospect's buying style. Using this method gives you the best chance for sales success. Complete information about the various approaches to understanding and matching buying styles can be found in *The New Strategic Selling* written by Miller and Heiman. The example given here is to present a simplified example of Miller-Heiman's approach.

Counselor Selling / The Partnership Approach

If we look at an article I wrote several years ago called "Green Light, Red Light, Yellow Light," we'll see the four basic sales styles.

See "Articles" at coachnickray.com.

The type one and type two sales styles are the basic high pressure sales people. Type three is the counselor seller and type four uses the partnership approach. Types three and four are quite familiar to people who understand counselor selling, which was introduced in the mid 70s by Larry Wilson. In any case, counselor selling and the partnership approach have two significant differences from types one and two:

1. In type three and four the advisor's fundamental interest is in discovering the problems the client or prospect is trying to solve. The emphasis is on serving the buyer, not just satisfying the seller's needs.
2. Additionally, the partnership approach is firmly grounded in the advisor's willingness to hear "No."

Type one and two are characterized by the seller trying to coerce the buyer into saying "yes." In the partnership approach, we are open to dealing with objections, as objections are a natural part of almost all sales interviews. Rather than fight this reality, it is more productive to have a strategy for dealing with objections. The partnership approach is a natural extension of counselor selling in that all the feelings of the buyer, especially hearing "no," are given appropriate regard.

Moving Forward – The Rule

Effective selling requires that you never proceed from one step to the next step in the sales process without having received 100% from the buyer to move forward. Consent can look like this: asking for more information, asking someone to take a physical exam for life insurance, or asking for permission to speak to anyone who may impact the buying decision. There are any number of important things that you might have to discover, the absence of which could sink the sale.

When you get consent to move forward at every step, your closing ratio will improve. When you have gained consent at each step in the sales process, you effectively qualify your prospect each step of the way. As objections and compromises are exposed in a timely fashion, closes only occur with truly interested buyers. Work on unproductive cases is stopped earlier in the sales process and unnecessary work is avoided.

No – Don't Hate the Word

Another tool to help you improve your closing ratio is to learn to deal with the concept of "no." First, identify which type of "no" you face, as discussed on page 75. If it's "no forever," exit with grace. If it's "no-for-now," the case is still alive.

To get a better explanation of this concept please see the book *Consultative Closing* written by Greg Bennett.

The Power Close – It's Not What You Think

How do you close? It's simple. You present the underlying assumptions of your recommendations and the solutions you believe will solve your prospect's problems. Then you ask: "Mr. or Ms. Prospect, what's our next step? Are you prepared to move forward at this time?" Compared to clever or high pressure techniques for closing, this simple close uses precisely the opposite approach. The reason you can do this is that if you've correctly followed all the steps outlined in this sales process, your closing presentation should be relatively simple.

There you have it. The close is relatively easy and also takes the least amount of time of any step in the sales process. But without successfully closing cases you won't stay in business. That is why, in the ranking of all the important activities in the sales process, closing the case and getting paid is the most important step. This step does not take the most time, but it is the step that has the greatest impact on your professional success.

Closing Ratio

As a salesperson you should know your closing ratio. One of the simplest ways you can measure this ratio is to use my CAPS Record Keeping Form discussed on page 53. CAPS = Contacts, Appointments, Presentations and Sales. If you keep this simple record of your activities, you're able to calculate your sales activity ratios. Careful analysis of these CAPS ratios can help you determine how and where to improve your sales effectiveness.

"CAPS" is available at SalesSolutionsPress.com.

As stated above, the closing interview should be the least surprising part of the sales process. If you experience surprises in a closing interview, you have not done your job well at an earlier step in the sales process; usually the breakdown usually occurs in the fact finding phase. That is why I am so emphatic that you always use a printed fact finder. A fact finder is the essential tool you need to help you gather all the information required to make a solid presentation.

When you have done your job correctly, your closing ratio should be 50% or better. The reason behind the improved ratio (it's usually about 33%) is that you will stop making presentations to people who are poor prospects. You will also stop making presentations hoping that somehow, some way, your persuasive skills will convince your prospect to buy from you, even if they are not a good prospect or you have not correctly identified their basic needs.

Getting Your Case Issued – The Underwriting Process

After a positive close, your next step is to have a well-documented system for completing the underwriting process. You will not be paid until your case has been issued. Some financial products have an extensive underwriting procedure. Life, health and disability products fall in this category, while non-insurance financial investments generally do not. After successfully closing the case, and especially when issuance of a case is not automatic, it's critical that you thoroughly and completely discuss the health and financial aspects of the underwriting process. Failure to do this often results in unwanted problems and delays, as well as anxiety on the advisor's part regarding issuance of the case.

For example, if you haven't gathered enough information about a person's health history, you could be in for a very, very big surprise even if your client is only 25 or 30. People have health issues even at young ages. When submitting the application to the insurance company, it's important to have discussed the insurance underwriting requirements with your client, and to have all the paperwork properly completed. Everything that you need to close the case should be on a checklist, which either you or your assistant can handle.

Using life insurance as an example, you should have the completed application, extensive medical history, a listing of all medications taken, height and weight information, and doctors that your client has seen. Just as you should have no surprises when closing the case, you should also have no surprises when a case goes into underwriting. Some products don't have much underwriting, but insurance policies can often entail a very complicated process. The underwriting process should be as well organized as any other part of your sales process; checklists and time deadlines are a critically important part of this process.

Delivering the Case – Do It Right

You've closed the case, you have been paid, and everything turned out well. You and your client are delighted. Another opportunity now awaits you. If your product requires any kind of explanation as to how it works, or has any kind of important legal characteristics, you should have a delivery checklist to explain these characteristics.

For example, assume that you sold a life insurance policy. You should have a formal delivery checklist, which describes all of the significant legal aspects of the policy: the contestable period, any policy exclusions, contractual limitations of any kind, policy premium payment options, and guaranteed and projected (non-guaranteed) policy values.

The product should be delivered in person if at all possible. I rarely, if ever, delivered a policy by mail. What's the reason for this? First of all, it's a value added service. The sale of a product and attentive follow-on service should include an explanation of all important product characteristics. Value added service can start with an explanation of the contractual provisions. A delivery receipt is provided; this receipt will be proof that the policy has been delivered and all of the significant aspects of the contract have been discussed. This extra step is a very good way to avoid any future conflicts about the policy. Give one copy of the delivery checklist to your client and keep one for your file. This extra service yields two bonuses: extra client loyalty and more client referrals.

For samples, see "Delivery Checklists" in Appendix 4.

One of the hardest things to do in the sales business is to get a new client. Taking good care of an existing client can be worth a fortune to you because good clients refer others who will also become good clients.

Keeping a Client Happy Leads to Having a Happy Client

In the delivery interview you should discuss the ongoing service(s) you'll be providing. You also need to explain who to contact if you're not available. Further, you should describe your client contact program you use to stay in contact with your clients. Successful advisors usually have 24-28 total contacts per year, with 2-4 of those contacts being face to face meetings with the client.

It is a mistake to think that the sales process begins with getting a referral and ends with making a sale. Effective sales people know that repeat business comes from giving good ongoing service to clients. As mentioned above, a delivery checklist is a good way to describe the product you've just sold and the ongoing service you'll provide.

Opening to Closing Highlights of the Sales Process

- Always complete a written fact finder.
- Always capture the names of future prospects.
- Discover the prospect's agenda and the prospect's concerns if his basic problems aren't solved.
- Deal with all objections before the closing appointment or you could be in store for surprises (not all being pleasant).
- Discover and talk to all members of your prospect's buying committee before the close.
- If possible, find an inside contact to provide accurate political and sales support information.
- Don't proceed from one sales step to the next without gaining 100% compliance to move forward from the buyer.
- Have all paperwork prepared in advance of the closing interview.
- Present your case in a summary fashion – include assumptions and recommendations. Place supporting documents in back of summary.
- Discuss every step of the process – manage expectations and requirements.
- Have a case file checklist with deadlines so that the case issuance is as smooth as possible.
- Set up the case delivery procedures and explain details to buyer. Discuss ongoing services, your regular contact program, referral conversations, and other products / services you provide.

NINE

Administrative Support Builds a Great Practice

Let's begin this chapter with a virtual trip to Nordstrom's – what will we see?

- An attractive, well-maintained store
- Attentive, helpful and well-trained sales associates
- Excellent merchandise
- Good business practices (such as a liberal return policy) that make shopping an easy and pleasant experience

The net result: a loyal clientele.

What won't we see?

- The sales associates being trained
- The building manager and his staff planning maintenance programs and training the maintenance people
- The buyers' travel and time spent selecting merchandise
- Long-term planning efforts carried out by senior staff

These behind-the-scenes efforts are built around a carefully executed business plan, with extensive training and performance reviews. All well-run companies work this way.

The Nordstrom's example reflects business mastery. According to Michael Masterson, who has studied great achievers, it takes about 5,000

See "Did Malcolm Gladwell Rip Me Off?" at earlytorise.com.

hours and 10 years to achieve mastery – it takes another 5000 hours to achieve virtuosity – assuming you have the inborn talent. The process of achieving mastery is generally not obvious. We merely see the results of focused effort and attention, as in the case of Nordstrom's.

For financial service professionals, the requirements for achieving mastery are similar to those faced by any other professional: focused effort over time. Yet the specific efforts necessary to achieve an effective and efficient practice can be elusive. In our effort to achieve mastery, we should keep these two goals in mind for our practice:

- We want an effective practice – doing the right things (strategy)
- We want an efficient practice – doing things right (tactics)

Whatever you do, the emphasis should first be on having the right strategy – then employing the right tactics.

The Unseen Part of a Great Practice

Thus far in this book we've talked about the direct responsibilities you have to your clients and prospects as a financial advisor or salesperson. The process described has been fairly linear. It began with eligibility and suitability guidelines for the financial services business, and then covered all the steps of the sales process itself. The purpose of this chapter is to provide an overview of the various aspects of what are called the "back office" or support operations.

With broad brushstrokes, let's describe the required tools for effective office support. My bibliography will also provide many additional sources for effective practice management.

Candidate Selection and Retention Process

An effective process requires that you master these 3 steps:

- Establish eligibility guidelines
- Establish suitability guidelines
- Implement effective interview procedures

Sales Training Program

Steps you need to take:

- Select a basic training program
- Institute a classroom / online learning program
- Institute a field sales training program which will include regular observation, regular feedback, and continuing motivation conversations

SALES TRAINING PROGRAM NOTES

Once a candidate is selected, the next critical agent success factor is the quality of the sales training program itself. Sales styles can fall into 1 of 4 categories: #1, the Huckster; #2, the Persuader; #3, the Problem Solver; and #4, the Partnership Approach.

The Huckster and the Persuader are examples of the outdated high-pressure selling system and are not recommended. A sales training program which depends upon manipulation or deception is not recommended.

See the "Green Light, Red Light, Yellow Light" article on the attached CD (or read it online at coachnickray.com/articles).

The Problem Solver and the Partnership Approach are the most productive sales styles for long-term success. These approaches should be fundamental in any sales training program you select. The training program should have two distinct parts. The first is formal sales training, typically done in a classroom style. The wide availability of electronically-based training is a popular alternative to a more traditional classroom-based training process, which often incurs high travel costs. The second distinct part is a 3-legged field sales coaching/training system that includes regular observation, thoughtful and helpful feedback, and continuous motivation. I have been surprised to discover that this hands-on aspect of sales training is almost exclusively noted for its absence. Effective sales training is actually regular sales coaching. Hiring candidates more carefully and training candidates more thoroughly will result in better morale, improved retention, and lower overall sales costs.

For more information about effective selling systems, see integritysystems.com.

Design a Usable Business Plan

Do you have a business plan? As a certified provider for the One Page Business Plan, I know the value of having a usable business plan.

The One Page Business Plan deals with the five basic aspects of any business:

PART I – The Foundation

1. Your vision
2. The mission for your business or practice

PART II – Implementing the Plan

3. Determine the measurable objectives you have for each business plan year
4. Select the strategies you will follow to make your objectives a reality
5. Implement the action plans you will use to achieve your desired objectives in a timely fashion

The One Page Business Plan is, as the title states, only one page long. It's the most effective tool I've seen to help people design and implement an actionable business plan. Fortunately, there is a program designed just for financial service advisors. The One Page Business Plan allows you to organize and implement a plan that, if followed, will help guarantee success in achieving your business objectives. I recommend that you and your key staff members complete a Plan.

See The One Page Business Plan at onepagebusiness-plan.com.

Here is an example of a well-aligned plan (for the first 3 steps) between an advisor and his or her assistant:

Advisor

VISION:

To generate $750,000 of revenue in the next 12 months by selling our preferred products to target market/ideal clients in the Bay area

MISSION:

Producing peace of mind and financial security

OBJECTIVES:

- Generate a breakeven budget by 12/31/XX
- Define my target market / ideal client
- Obtain 15 ideal client referrals per month
- Open 6 new ideal client cases per month
- Close 2 new ideal clients per month

Advisor's Assistant

VISION:

To serve our clients by relieving my boss of all non-income producing tasks

MISSION:

To provide secure, dependable sales and administrative back-up for all my boss's needs

OBJECTIVES:

- Assemble all data for breakeven budget by 12/15/XX
- Work with my boss to identify and assemble ideal client list
- Follow and meet referral lead system requirements every week
- Prepare new client kits 1 day prior to each interview
- Make sure all forms, presentation material and proposals are delivered on time

Action Blueprint

Successful financial service professionals achieve their objectives by completing this three-step process to achieve their business objectives. These three steps are Part II of the One Page Business Plan listed above.

Step 1: State the objective – *what* you'll do

Step 2: State the strategy – *how* you'll do it

Step 3: Describe your action plan – *when* you'll do it

ONE PAGE BUSINESS PLAN EXAMPLE

Objective: Implement a referred lead prospecting program.

Strategy: Perfect my referred lead program by reading *10 Steps to Building a Referred Lead Engine*; studying the workbook; and revising my fact finder to help me capture names of future prospects.

Action Plan: Begin using the revised fact finder and record the number of names captured and referrals received. Keep records on a weekly basis.

See sample One Page Business Plans in Appendix 4 on page 148.

You must be clear about your objective, select strategies or methods you'll use to achieve your objective, and then implement an action plan to achieve your objective in a timely fashion. You can use this sample 3-step process to achieve any business or personal goal.

Discover Your Target Market: Put It in Writing

See the *Invisible Market Matrix* to discover your natural target market at SalesSolutionsPress.com.

After you discover your target market profile, you and your staff will have a very clear idea about who has chosen to work with you and why. Knowing this, you can gear your marketing efforts and client interaction protocols to accommodate the people who like you and are most enjoyable for you to work with. Having a clearly defined target market will also allow you to customize your marketing efforts and select those marketing channels that yield the best results.

Designing Useful Fact Finders

Available at toolsformoney.com.

Excellent fact finders and proposal templates are available from Tools for Money. These are probably the best fact finders that I've found. They can be customized to fit your exact needs, and are very fairly priced. As they are Word documents, they can also be very easily changed or modified to suit your needs. This is an important benefit as too many fact finders ask poorly designed or unnecessaryquestions and thus end up being unused.

Prospecting and Marketing Duties

As previously discussed, you need to decide what type of marketing channels you will use. Next, you should have a specific and well designed prospecting and marketing program, which means that you have to determine what your target market profile is and how you'll reach members of your target market.

From an administrative standpoint, it's important to determine which marketing tasks are assigned to whom. While you are responsible for most of the prospecting and marketing duties, your staff can assist with many of them. The following chart gives you an idea of how you might share the tasks.

COORDINATING MARKETING AND PROSPECTING EFFORTS WITH YOUR ADMINISTRATIVE STAFF

ACTIVITY	ADVISOR	STAFF
Capture client's compelling issues from the fact finder	X	
Ask for client referrals	X	
Set up Center of Influence relationships	X	
Maintain Center of Influence relationships	X	X
Set up Center of Service networking system	X	
Maintain Center of Service networking system	X	X
Maintain Center of Service relationships	X	X
Do regular marketing mailings		X
Call clients	X	X*
Call Center of Influence referrals	X	X*
Call Center of Service referrals	X	X*
Send referrers thank you notes / gifts		X
Follow up with referrals and referrers about outcomes	X	X
Monitor and evaluate referral records	X	X

*This may be a shared responsibility.

Sales Process Steps

- Develop an initial contact process (asking for the initial interview)
- Develop and use an Initial Interview Questionnaire
- Develop and use a printed fact finder
- Develop and use a buying committee fact finder
- Understand your prospect's buying styles
- Determine buyer's critical issues/desire to solve problems now
- Develop standardized sales presentations, reflecting your prospect/client's buying style
- Develop standard closing procedures

Heiman, Miller and Teluja.

The marketing process ends and the sales process begins when you make the initial contact with a potential prospect. The sales process ends when the sale is made and you have been paid. It's important to note that client contact does not end after you've sold the case and been paid – it's just that the sales process has ended.

Foundational issues in the sales process are to have a very clear idea of your product / service offering; a simple and easy process for discovering whether you can be of service to the prospect; and a process that guarantees that all the steps in the sales process will be covered. Further, we know that systematizing all the steps in the sales process enhances your effectiveness (you're asking the right questions) and efficiency (you're doing things right).

Financial and Insurance Planning Software

- Financial Planning software
- Insurance Planning software
- Sales presentation software
- Rebalancing software
- Portfolio management software

For those in the financial advisory business, there is an extensive range of sales and planning software available. The most basic is software designed to produce a financial plan and/or an insurance plan. These two pieces of software are fundamental in any financial advisory business.

It's worth mentioning, again, that your life will be made much simpler if the input screen data for your presentation software are collected in your printed fact finder. I don't believe there is anything more embarrassing than having to go back to a busy prospect and ask for information you should have collected the first time around. If your fact finder does not have room for all your software input data needed, then you should carry supplemental fact finders for your presentation software. For those who work in the securities end of the advisory business, rebalancing software and portfolio management software are often essential components of your practice.

GOAL-BASED FINANCIAL PLANNING SOFTWARE

The emphasis is on the end result.

- Money Tree
- MoneyGuide Pro
- E-money Advisor

CASH-FLOW BASED FINANCIAL PLANNING SOFTWARE

The emphasis here is detailed, year-by-year cash flow analyses.

- NaviPlan Extended
- Advisor Workbench
- Financial Profiles

SALES PRESENTATION SOFTWARE

A good place to start is to contact your current vendors and obtain compliance approved software.

REBALANCING SOFTWARE

For advisors using stocks, ETFs, mutual funds, and other investment products, consider:

- ASI: asipartner.com
- eAllocator: eAllocator.com
- iRebal: irebal.com
- Tamarac: tamaracinc.com

For more information, see advisormax.com.

For additional information about software support, visit Technology Tools for Today (T3), technologytoolsfortoday.com. This newsletter is highly recommended and allows you to receive the latest news on virtual office tools and technology. It is written by David Drucker and Joel Bruckenstein.

PORTFOLIO MANAGEMENT SOFTWARE

- Schwab's Portfolio Center
- Advent
- Albridge

Practice Management Software

- Select and use a CRM system
- Implement a compliance program for all sales and administrative procedures
- One little used but very helpful record keeping system is sales inventory / pipeline measurement systems. If you discover that your inventory, or pipeline, is diminishing, you can improve your marketing activities accordingly.
- Document management software
- Document authentication software
- Digital client statements

Other helpful software includes: paperless office procedures, digital client statements software, document authentication software, and software that addresses computer safety issues.

CRM SOFTWARE

- Advisor's Assistant: advisorsassistant.com (in-house and web-based)
- SmartOffice: ez-data.com (web-based only)
- Red Tail
- Gold Mine
- ACT! for Advisors

COMPLIANCE SYSTEM INFORMATION

Read Nancy Lininger's article "The Art of Compliance." She can be reached at liftburden.com/contact_nancy.htm. Her article can be found at coachnickray.com, or in the CD included with this book.

DOCUMENT MANAGEMENT SOFTWARE

You should consider LaserFiche, Cabinet NG, and DocuXplorer.

DOCUMENT AUTHENTICATION SOFTWARE

You should consider ProofSpace and Xerox.

DIGITAL CLIENT STATEMENTS

You should consider Trumpet Inc, Assemblage, and CRM Software's ClientView.

AUTOMATIC FORM COMPLETION AND KEEPING FORMS CURRENT SOFTWARE

LaserApp.com is a company which markets automatic form completion software and integrates it with Advisor Assistant CRM software. See Advisors Assistant for more information, advisorsassistant.com.

COMPUTER SAFETY ISSUES

- Select appropriate Anti-virus / Firewall / Anti-spam / Spyware software
- Have computer data back-up systems in place
- Have computer stand-by/emergency power systems for all computers

Administrative Resources

3 INTERESTING BOOKS

The E-Myth Revisited, by Michael E. Gerber, describes in interesting detail how you can run your business like a business. *Tested in the Trenches: A 9-Step Plan for Building and Sustaining a Million-Dollar Financial Services Practice,* by Ron Carson and Steve Sanduski, provides an entire system of forms you can use to run your practice more efficiently. Peter and Katherine Vessenes' book, *Building Your Multimillion Dollar Practice: 8 Success Strategies of Top Producing Advisors,* is another good source for how a well-run office operates.

ACCOUNTING SOFTWARE

For accounting software, QuickBooks and Microsoft Money are good sources and are widely available. If you are a financial services advisor in the securities field, you may also need to have portfolio management software. For people interested in sophisticated software in the financial advisory business, my recommendation is the newsletter "Technology Tools for Today (t3)" for the future of office technology.

Available at technologytools-fortoday.com.

SALES RECORDS

These records can be kept electronically or they can be paper-based. Sales Activity Management Incorporated is a good source for paper-based record keeping books. Their standard forms are excellent. Customized records are also available.

Available at salesactivity-management.com, or see "CAPS" at SalesSolutionsPress.com.

KEEP TRACK OF YOUR PROFIT AND LOSS

You should be producing a monthly profit/loss statement and a quarterly or semiannual balance sheet. Every successful business keeps good records. The monthly profit/loss statement should be based on a concept called the 'breakeven' budget process. Many advisors believe they're successful because they have money in the bank at the end of the month, after having paid all their bills. This is an incomplete way of

See "The Breakeven Budget" at SalesSolutionsPress.com.

looking at your business. The 'breakeven' for any business is based upon accounting for all of the following factors:

1. Your base salary.
2. The salaries of everyone who works for you.
3. All your commission and employee bonus expenses.
4. All of your other fixed expenses.
5. Your monthly breakeven point has to include all predictable but variable expenses such as quarterly bills and expenses committed to specific projects.
6. Your breakeven point should also cover marketing expenditures that are part of your business plan.
7. It should include retirement plan costs for you and your employees.
8. It should include any other insurance expenses you have in your practice.
9. It should include reserve funds to cover unexpected costs, emergency expenses, and funds to cover you in an economic downturn. A six to twelve month reserve fund is a reasonable goal.

Only after you have met all of your fixed and variable costs – most of which are predictable and some of which are not – can you determine if you've made a profit. Even if you have cash in your checking account at the end of the month, that money is not yours for the taking, unless you know you have met all of your other financial obligations. These financial obligations maintain and sustain the profitability of your business over the long haul. That is why your monthly profit / loss statement should account for all of these factors, not just whether you've covered your immediate bills.

Other Important Administrative Procedures

Administrative procedures may be the biggest back office issue any advisor faces. This is the area almost no one sees (except you and your staff), yet a successful back office operation is the key to a successful practice. Without good back office practices, you won't have the time to engage in those necessary marketing activities that assure your continued business success.

You should have well-defined job descriptions for everyone who works for you, including yourself. This could be as simple as a notebook where daily job responsibilities are listed. According to Katherine and Peter Vessenes, there could be some complicated procedures with as many as 700 to 1000 steps. I know that may seem like an overwhelming number, but think about the sales process that we've just discussed and you can see that there are many, many steps that you need to complete to process a sale or make any administrative change. The requirement is that you have office operations well documented, so that you'll cover all your bases efficiently.

Vessenes, 56.

EMPLOYEE PROCEDURES

- Develop a written job description or job manual for each position
- Provide continuous employee training
- Conduct regular employee performance reviews
- Establish salary and bonus policies
- Provide employee benefit annual statements

support@BSIweb.com

SETTING UP SEAMLESS ADMINISTRATIVE PROCEDURES – IT TAKES TIME

Most administrative procedures should be invisible to your clients / prospects. All clients should see is the end result of your office procedures. It reminds me of that old saying, "Laws are like sausages – it is better not to see them being made." (John Godfrey Saxe, 1869).

Your clients don't want to see what you go through in order to put a process together. They just want to know that you are responsive, and that you and your staff provide the answers they need in a timely fashion. They don't care how you do it, but they will complain if you don't handle administrative procedures well. In my experience, it may take 1-2 years to set up all the recommended office procedures to your satisfaction; maintenance is an ongoing process.

TELEPHONE AND E-MAIL ETIQUETTE AND STANDARDS

The most vexing daily issue for most advisors is the telephone. That is why you should have procedures for how you deal with clients, such as your telephone call response time. Based on my experience, the maximum response time for returning calls is 2-3 hours. I suspect advisors lose more clients due to slow telephone and e-mail response time than any other reason. In a business where it's often difficult to distinguish products or advisory services, one factor easily identified is the time it takes to return your calls and e-mails.

In my opinion, automated voice answering machines are the worst thing to have ever happened to businesses that claim, "Service is our most important product," or, "Our customers are our most valuable asset." If you are in a service business and depend on referrals for new clients, dump automated answering – go back to real people answering your telephone. Then, train your people on answering calls, transferring calls, handling complaints, and making sure messages are delivered in a timely fashion. Of course, voice mail used after hours is fine, or when the caller wants to leave a message for a person not available at the time.

An Administrative Checklist – How Are You Doing?

Give yourself a score with "1" indicating never and "6" indicating always.

I use a printed fact finder.	1 2 3 4 5 6
I have an effective fact finding program.	1 2 3 4 5 6
My administrative procedures are written down and each administrative position has its own procedures manual.	1 2 3 4 5 6
I have a well-defined target market.	1 2 3 4 5 6
I have a well-defined ideal client.	1 2 3 4 5 6
I have a useful and actionable One Page Business Plan.	1 2 3 4 5 6
I revise my business plan on an annual basis.	1 2 3 4 5 6
I have a CRM system.	1 2 3 4 5 6
I use my CRM system on a regular basis.	1 2 3 4 5 6
I have a policy / product delivery system that I use for all of my products on a regular basis.	1 2 3 4 5 6
I have standardized file folders for my clients.	1 2 3 4 5 6
I have standardized procedures that I use when opening a case.	1 2 3 4 5 6
All of the data that I collect fits neatly into all of my software at my office (I only have to collect data once to make my system work effectively).	1 2 3 4 5 6
Each of my key employees has a business plan that is aligned with my business plan.	1 2 3 4 5 6
People understand the income program we have in our office and how bonuses are paid.	1 2 3 4 5 6

We have well-designed and well-integrated graphic materials, including letterhead, business cards, signage, presentation pages, report forms, etc.	1 2 3 4 5 6
I have and use a breakeven budget.	1 2 3 4 5 6

Running a successful business requires creating a team of people to seamlessly handle the variety of "behind-the-scenes" work. By following clear principles and keeping your eye on the vision, mission and objectives of your business or practice, you are sure to provide the necessary support for each and every sale. Smooth daily operations will bring confidence to each client who contacts your office. Positive office interactions will foster goodwill and affect how you pursue your next sale, ultimately leading to broader success.

The behind-the-scenes support that employees provide is a critically important factor in building a successful financial practice. Most financial advisors are not fond of paperwork or details in general. In my experience, advisors would do well to delegate responsibility to employees to maintain records and track data, enabling them to pursue further marketing opportunities. We know that good employees make our life much simpler, more pleasurable, and more profitable.

TEN

A Comprehensive Assessment

In Chapter One we asked this question: Are you, and the industry you find yourself in, a good fit? On the assumption that the answer was yes, you're now in the position to evaluate just how good a job you've done as a financial services professional. The test for success is a broad one; it is not simply whether you've earned a good income. What's important is what you have done with that income, and what kind of life you have made for yourself, your employees, and the people you love and care for.

Too often the only measure of success used is your financial success. But in this book the basic concepts behind the test for success are broader. Have you treated your clients well? Have you treated your employees well? Have you treated your family well? Have you treated yourself well? The most successful person will be able to say yes to each of these questions.

Your Personal Life Assessment

In this chapter we want to evaluate what it means to be a success from a financial as well as a personal and, ultimately, life affirming point of view.

Financial Success

The first question is: have you made enough money to support yourself (and your family, if you have one) in a style which you find acceptable? But more than that, ask yourself: have I managed my own financial affairs as well as I have managed the financial affairs of my clients? Your own personal measure of financial success can be evaluated by answering these questions:

- Have you lived within your means?
- Have you limited your personal debts to a house and perhaps a car, and avoided debt for normal day-to-day purchases?
- Do you have zero long-term credit card debt? I find nothing wrong with using a credit card so long as you pay it off at the end of each month. A credit card should be viewed as a financial convenience, and not as a means to pursue an unaffordable or unsustainable lifestyle.
- Do you manage your budget well enough so that you cover all your current expenses without borrowing?
- Have you funded your children's college education to the extent you're capable of and interested in?
- Have you managed your debts properly?
- Do you have a comprehensive retirement program that will allow you to retire in comfort without undue concern about the impact of inflation?
- Does your retirement program include funding specifically to cover long-term care costs (either enough cash or long term care insurance)?
- Do you have adequate funding for estate taxes, charitable contributions, and inheritances you wish to leave?

A useful tool to determine funding availability is "The Breakeven Budget," available at SalesSolutionsPress.com.

As this book is being written we are just beginning to emerge from the most severe financial crisis since the Great Depression. Due regard should be given to the short-term impact on your overall financial affairs.

CONSIDER YOUR EMPLOYEES

Another aspect of running a successful financial practice is to evaluate how well you've treated your employees. In my career I've known some advisors and business owners who didn't care for their employees at all, whereas other employers made sure that their employees were able to retire with 70-80% of their pre-retirement income.

My expectation is that employees should have the same percentage of retirement income as I have for myself. When completing your business plan, you should consider your employees your most valuable asset; as such, you should provide them with the same level of care and benefits you provide for yourself.

SELLING YOUR PRACTICE

If your financial and your personal affairs are in order, another measure of managing a successful retirement is arranging for the sale of your business or practice in an orderly fashion. What are your choices when transferring your practice?

- You can simply close your doors
- You can sell all your real property – an asset sale – and then close your doors.
- You can assign or give clients to another advisor.
- If you have an ongoing, assignable flow of income (commissions, fees, trails, etc.), you are in a more favorable financial position, because you have something to sell: an income stream.

When I left my practice, I only had my group practices to sell. My life / DI practice quickly became renewals only, and my life clients yielded only split first-year commissions when new life sales were made. In any case, it is highly recommended that you consult with a practice evaluation service as well as a business attorney to ensure that the practice evaluation is fair and the sales agreement is equitable and legally enforceable.

See FPTransitions.com, a Portland, Oregon-based practice valuations company.

LOOK FOR A SOLID BUYER

Many practice sales are, in effect, leveraged buyouts. This simply means that the buyer purchased your practice out of the income stream your practice provides. This method may present problems.

For instance, if the buyer manages your practice poorly, how will you be paid if the practice falters? As is well known, you can't get blood from a turnip, so your income from the sale could stop if your buyer manages the practice poorly and hasn't sufficient income to pay you.

One solution is to check your buyer's credit rating thoroughly so that you only sell to credit-worthy buyers. Another is to make sure you get a significant down payment in cash. You should have fewer problems selling a 7-figure practice, as buyers of this size practice are usually more solid financially. Most buy-out difficulties occur with smaller practices.

Look for buyers of excellent character with a good track record and solid net worth. "Trust – and verify."

Adequate Retirement Funding

Living in an affluent society provides us with the choice of a comfortable and secure lifestyle, but it doesn't happen automatically and it isn't cheap! Excluding Social Security benefits, I think that adequate retirement funding takes at least 15% to 20% of your annual income. You should start in your 20s, or as soon as your income stabilizes. My motto: pay yourself first!

Thus, a person making $200,000 per year may pay about $40,000 in income tax. Of the $160,000 remaining, about $30,000 should be invested for various types of retirement programs. That amount can include permanent life insurance, qualified retirement plans, and other long-term investments.

Admittedly this is a conservative approach, but it can be very unsettling to retire, only to discover that you have inadequate funds to maintain your desired lifestyle. The ultimate test of running your business successfully is whether you've managed your life and your financial affairs successfully. Measuring your success only on how much money you've made is an incomplete evaluation of your personal and financial success.

A more complete measure of success should include leaving a positive legacy: Not only do you want to pass on a financial legacy where your loved ones are provided for, but a personal legacy where your desire to do good in the world begins with peaceful bonds between family members and reconciliation wherever possible. Discord in families often results in squandering an inheritance to legal costs, as well as leaving people with bitter and unhappy thoughts.

A SAD LIFE INSURANCE STORY

Many years ago a business life insurance client of mine (a doctor) died, and his widow called me to help her figure out how much personal life insurance her husband had left her. He was seventy-three and had died suddenly of ruptured aortic aneurysms. His wife was about sixty-five. They had a home in Southern California and a beach home she was planning to live in when she and her husband retired.

An appointment was set to help her review her husband's life insurance program. The widow brought out a large box of insurance policies and asked me to help her determine which policies were in force.

The system I used was to throw the policies no longer in force on the floor and leave policies in force on the table. So began the selection process. About twenty minutes later we had one policy on the table – with a face amount of $100,000 – and about thirty or forty policies on the floor.

Her husband was obviously not a believer in personal life insurance planning or permanent life insurance. That is why he never agreed to talk to me about his personal life insurance program. As I discovered, his life insurance planning system was simple and inadequate: he would buy association term life insurance coverage and just replace it with a new policy when a new offer came, which was every year. This explains how he had purchased maybe thirty or forty policies, only one of which was in force at his death. It would not be an understatement to say that this widow was in a state of shock and severe disappointment regarding her husband's meager life insurance program.

She was not bereft of funds, but her desire to live in the beach house near Santa Barbara was no longer a possibility. After all her debts were paid off, there was only enough money for her to live in a condominium in the Los Angeles area, but not at her beautiful beach house near the ocean.

Some of you may ask, "What's the problem in this situation? The widow was not broke!" But if this couple's plans were to provide an inheritance for heirs, provide sufficient funds to maintain a comfortable lifestyle for a surviving spouse or partner, and have sufficient retirement income for both surviving partners, then their planning clearly was inadequate.

LONG-TERM CARE FUNDING

We need to ask one more question: do you have sufficient long-term care insurance to provide financial security in the event that you and / or your spouse or partner needs continuing care?

The reason is that financing long-term care is expensive. In today's dollars it could be $60,000 to $70,000 per year. You would want to be able to maintain your normal standard of living even if you had this extra expenditure thrust upon you, and it lasted for five or even ten years. Long-term care insurance is a fundamental part of a good retirement plan.

Final Arrangements

I believe the discussion of funeral arrangements and the disposition of your assets should be handled when you are of sound mind and body. Handling these issues may fill you with trepidation. Perhaps relationships are better with some family members than others. The time to deal with these personal and financial issues is when you're well, not when you're ill. My suggestion is simple: no loose ends. Make sure that you've covered the important personal and financial matters with family members while you are still in good enough shape to handle this discussion in a responsible fashion.

RESOLVE YOUR DIFFERENCES

Another factor to consider is how to handle estrangement between you and other family members, children or siblings. Should this be an issue, now would be a good time to resolve these differences. I'm not suggesting that you suddenly become best friends with people with whom you've had significant differences, but it makes life a little easier if you work to resolve your differences before it's too late.

LEGAL DOCUMENTS

You'd want to make sure that all your important legal documents are current by asking these questions:

- Are your will and trust documents up to date?
- Do you have an up-to-date health directive and a durable power of attorney?
- Have you organized your financial and legal affairs so that at your death or disability the people caring for you will know where all your paperwork is located?
- Have you gone over your legal documents and the disposition of your assets with those who are closest to you? This conversation will reduce or even eliminate the nature and amount of family arguments and discord after you've died.

Ideally, there will not be the scene in the lawyer's office where all the family members have gathered, each of whom is hoping to get a substantial inheritance, only to discover that the deceased has left all of his or her money to the local Humane Society. If it's your intention to leave your money to charity, and not to family members, it shouldn't be a surprise to those who are close to you when your assets are distributed.

A Well-Rounded Approach

Another measure of how well you run your business and manage your life is to evaluate your own physical and emotional health. This means that you would have:

- Financial security
- Good physical health
- Emotional health and well-being

Use these standards to measure your degree of success.

In this chapter I am also saying that the test of success is not just what other people think of you; nor is it the reputation you've built; but rather, how well you've managed the totality of your life. And it's important to see your life as a series of inner connected processes:

- Your financial affairs
- Your health and physical well-being
- The quality of your relationships
- How well you treat your employees
- How well you've planned for your retirement
- How well organized your personal affairs are
- Whether you have a sufficient long-term care insurance program to cover long-term care needs
- The value of life insurance and other assets you will leave to your children and other family members
- Sufficient liquidity to cover transfer costs at death
- An estate plan which provides for the charitable contributions which are important to you

Your Lifestyle Checklist

Give yourself a score with "1" indicating poor and "6" indicating outstanding.

Are you earning a sufficient amount of income to provide the desired lifestyle for yourself and your family?	1 2 3 4 5 6
Are you providing an adequate amount of life insurance protection for those depending on you?	1 2 3 4 5 6
Do you have enough disability income protection to cover yourself if you are unable to work?	1 2 3 4 5 6
Do you provide your employees with a reasonable level of income?	1 2 3 4 5 6
Do you live within your means?	1 2 3 4 5 6

Are you debt free except for a home and (perhaps) a car?	1 2 3 4 5 6
Have you set aside sufficient money to provide a satisfactory level of income at your retirement?	1 2 3 4 5 6
Have you set aside sufficient retirement funds for your employees to retire comfortably?	1 2 3 4 5 6
Do you have well-drawn will and trust arrangements?	1 2 3 4 5 6
Do you have arrangements set up if you have a special needs child?	1 2 3 4 5 6
Have you completed a comprehensive insurance review to determine if you have an adequate amount of life and disability income insurance?	1 2 3 4 5 6
Do you have sufficient long-term care insurance?	1 2 3 4 5 6
Do you have sufficient liquidity to cover your estate at death?	1 2 3 4 5 6
Have you set aside sufficient funds for charity, should that be your desire, at your death?	1 2 3 4 5 6
Have you completed a P+C audit to assure that all your liability coverage is adequate and up-to-date?	1 2 3 4 5 6
Have you resolved the differences between friends, parents, siblings and children so that if you died tomorrow your personal relationships would be in good shape?	1 2 3 4 5 6
Is your life in proper balance? Is there a good balance between the amount of time that you work, you play, and you spend with your family?	1 2 3 4 5 6

A Final Note

Lao Tse said: "A journey of a thousand miles must begin with a single step."

In this book I have provided a myriad of guidelines, instructions, checklists and recommendations for you. Each of them can be helpful in improving your practice and enhancing your career. The dilemma faced by many is: Where to start?

Truthfully, any place you start will be helpful, because any improvement – large or small – will benefit your overall business. The key is simply to start. Pick a simple project and begin today to outline your plan of action. The Japanese word for "continuous improvement," *kaizen*, can be a useful mindset to move you into strategizing a new sales approach and a new life approach.

Appendices

Appendix 1: Fact Finder

Nick Ray Confidential Fact Finder

Page 1

Today's Date____________ Referred by:____________

Section 1. Personal / Business Information

Full name ____________

Nickname ____________ DOB____________

Home Address____________

City / State / Zip ____________

Business Address____________

City / State / Zip ____________

How long in this job? ____________ years This profession?____________ years

Company Name ____________

Job title / description____________

Do you report to anyone? ☐ Yes ☐ No

If so, what is their name and title? ____________

Married? ☐ Yes ☐ No Significant other / partner? ☐ Yes ☐ No

Spouse's Name____________ Sig. Other / Partner's Name ____________

How long? ____________ years How long? ____________ years

Children? ☐ Yes ☐ No Est. Income this year $ ____________ Last year $____________

Names / ages: 1. ____________ 2. ____________ 3.____________

Marriage anniversary: ____________

Section 2. Health / Physical Fitness Information

Please describe your exercise program ____________

____

Please describe your typical sleep pattern: average night's sleep, normal bedtime, quality of sleep / sleep meds?

____

Please list any health issues / medications (prescription / OTC) being taken: ____________

____

Height ____________ Weight____________ Weight Change in Last Year? ☐ Yes ☐ No Amount____________

Smoke? ☐ Yes ☐ No How long? ____________

CFF/07-10

Section 3. Marketing / Prospecting Information

Do you have a well-defined Target Market? ☐ Yes ☐ No What is your Target Market? ____________

How did you discover your Target Market? ______________________________

Describe the products / services you offer: ______________________________

____

Do you prospect on a regular basis? ☐ Yes ☐ No

Describe your referral source(s): ☐ Clients / Prospects ☐ COI ☐ Networks ☐ Other

Referral Information

How many referrals do you need each month? From Clients / Prospects ________ From COI ________

From Networks__________ From Other Sources__________

Are you meeting your referral goals? C / P: ☐ Yes ☐ No COI: ☐ Yes ☐ No NW: ☐ Yes ☐ No

Other: ☐ Yes ☐ No

Please describe the process you use to contact your referred leads: ______________________

Do you give as many referrals as you receive from COI and Network sources? ☐ Yes ☐ No

Network Marketing Information

Do you belong to any organizations serving your Target Market? ______________________

Do you receive any referrals from members of these organizations? ______________________

Do you have a relationship with Centers of Service serving your Target Market? ______________

Section 4. Fact Finder / Presentation Information

Do you use a printed Fact Finder? ☐ Yes ☐ No

How frequently do you use your printed Fact Finder? ☐ Always ☐ Sometimes ☐ Rarely

Does your Fact Finder capture the names of important personal and professional relationships? ☐ Yes ☐ No

Does your Fact Finder provide you with all the input data your CRM and presentation software require?

☐ Yes ☐ No

What kind of presentation software do you use? ______________________________

Do you use compliance-approved proposals for all of your sales presentations? ☐ Yes ☐ No

CFF/07-10

Section 5. Business / Practice Information

Section A – Business Plan

Do you have a business plan? ☐ Yes ☐ No

If yes, please describe the benefits your plan provides: ______________________________

How long have you been using a business plan? ______________________________

How often do you revise your business plan?

Section B – CRM Information

What kind of CRM software do you use? ____________________ How long: ____________

Is it PC-based or web-based? ☐ PC ☐ Web

Does your printed Fact Finder collect all the information that your CRM system requires? ☐ Yes ☐ No

List other software you use: ______________________________

Section C – Accounting Information

Are your accounting records completed electronically? ☐ Yes ☐ No

What type of accounting software do you use? ______________________________

☐ Complete In-House ☐ Completed by CPA, Bookkeeper

Do you produce a monthly profit and loss statement? ☐ Yes ☐ No

Do you produce a balance sheet on a regular basis? ☐ Yes ☐ No How Often? ☐ Q ☐ SA ☐ A

Do you use the Breakeven Budget Process? ☐ Yes ☐ No

Do you fund your retirement plan every year? ☐ Yes ☐ No

Section D – Sales Activity Records

Do you keep sales records? ☐ Yes ☐ No

List types of information you record: ______________________________

Are your results satisfactory? ☐ Yes ☐ No

Section E – Personnel Policies

Number of Administrative Staff: ______________________________

Do you have a printed procedures manual? ☐ Yes ☐ No

List the type of regular training you provide: ______________________________

CFF/07-10

Section 6. Coaching / Assessment History

Your coaching history and results: ______________________________

____

Have you completed any assessment instruments? ☐ Yes ☐ No If yes, which ones? ______________

____

Date(s) Taken: ______________________________

Did you find the results helpful? ☐ Yes ☐ No

If yes, please describe the benefits you derived: ______________________________

Section 7. Important Coaching Issues

Please list the 5 most importatnt issues you'd like to work on and the time frame you have in mind.

	Issue / Outcome	Time Frame
1.		
2.		
3.		
4.		
5.		

Other Coaching Issues

☐ Coaching Agreements

☐ Person Being Called Coach: Responsibility for completing assignments

☐ Fees: Late / Missed Appointments

☐ Periodic Reviews: Evaluating coaching program effectiveness

☐ Getting Things Done: What / By When

Coaching Fees

To cover fees, our normal procedure is to charge your Visa or Master Card account at the beginning of each month. An e-mail is sent to you confirming each charge.

FEES: **One Time: $ ________ Monthly: $ ________ # of Months: ____________**
Total: $ ___________

Coaching Timing

Date Sessions Begin: __________ # of Total Sessions: ________ # of Sessions / Month: ________

CFF/07-10

☐ Visa ☐ Master Card Card # ____________________ Exp. date:____/____

Name as it appears on card ____________________

Billing address for the card ____________________

City / State / Zip ____________________

Your e-mail address ____________________

Signature ____________________

Section 8. Contact Information

Home phone ____________________

Work phone ____________________

Cell phone ____________________

Fax ____________________

E-mail ____________________ Business Website ____________________

Preferred contact ____________________

CFF/07-10

Appendix 2: Sample Referral Logs

REFERRALS RECEIVED

Name of referral	Name of referror	In my Target Market Y/N	Sale Made Y/N	Thank you given to referror Y/N / Date	Feedback given to referror Y/N Date

REFERRALS GIVEN

Name of referral	Referred to / business or profession	Follow up call to referral Y/N / Date	Follow up call to person referred to Y/N / Date	Sale made to referral Y/N	Is referral in my Target Market? Y/N	Gift Received from person referred to Y/N

Appendix 3: Advanced 20-Point Days Checklist

If you want to change the results you're currently getting, you've got to change the things that you're currently doing. The 20-point day is a great way of "measuring" your day. This plan helps you when you need to get things back in balance… immediately. If you're serious about your business, this checklist can be a very useful tool.

VALUE	TASK
1 point	Making a telephone call to arrange a selling appointment.
2 points	Making the call and actually setting the appointment;
	setting the appointment any other way also counts 2 points.
2 points	Obtaining a "qualified" referral.
3 points	Delegating something that must be done… but not by you. Maximum 3 points / day.
3 points	Casework – it is either completed and ready to present to the client / prospect, or you accomplish a major step to significantly advance a case.
4 points	Conducting a face-to-face business meeting, regardless of the outcome. Opportunities arise from activity with prospective buyers / clients.
5 points	Attending an FPA, NAIFA, Rotary, Chamber or Commerce meeting (or similar community meeting) where you enhance your professional image. Maximum 5 points / day.
5 points	Completing the sale; an application is signed.
5 points	Exercising for longer than 30 minutes… if you do not stay healthy, the rest doesn't much matter.
10 points	Meeting with a Center of Influence: CPA, Attorney, P&C agent, business manager, etc.
20 points	Completing a sale on which the annualized revenue is in excess of your total daily objective (for example, over $1,500 annual commission).

NOTE: Tomorrow you start all over! There is no carryover. Make each day count. Good Luck!

"Success is nothing more than a few simple disciplines, practiced every day; while failure is simply a few errors in judgement,repeated every day. It is the cumulative weight of our disciplines and our judgements that leads us to either fortune or failure." – Jim Rohn

Advanced 20-Point Day Score Card

TASK	POINTS	M	T	W	T	F	SA	SU
Selling appointment call – attempt	1							
Selling appointment call – made (any method)	2							
Obtaining qualified referral	2							
Delegating task (max. 3 pts/day)	3							
Casework – either a major task completed or case ready for presentation	3							
Conducting a face- to-face business meeting	4							
Attending a community meeting	5							
Obtaining a signed application	5							
Exercising more than 30 minutes	5							
Meeting with a Center of Influence	10							
Completing sales in excess of daily goal	20							
Daily Total								
Weekly Total								

Appendix 4: Delivery Checklists

Contract Delivery Checklist

Estate Whole Life with Adjustable Protection
Premier Non-Tobacco Premium Class

Insurance Carrier: ____________________

Insured: ____________________

Policy Number: ____________________

Policy Date: ____________________

Date of Issue: ____________________

Create Dollars for Future Delivery

1. Death Benefit $ __________
2. Cash Values
   - 5 years $ __________
   - 10 years $ __________
   - Age 80 $ __________
3. Total Death Benefit at Age 80 $ __________

Values are based on the current dividend scale of 6.5% and assume dividends are used to purchase paid up additions and there are no policy loans .... [ ]

The Contract

1. Incontestability: Satisfied under Policy No. ____________________
2. Suicide: Satisfied under Policy No. ____________________
3. Owner: ____________________
4. Beneficiary: ____________________
5. Grace period, 31 days for emergency use only
6. Use of dividends – purchase paid up additions
7. Loans – automatic premium loan; 8% loan rate guaranteed

.... [ ]

Waiver of Premium - Not Applied for

.... [ ]

Policy Received by ____________________ Date __________

Your Company / Name
and Contact Information

Contract Delivery Checklist

Term to Age 80 – Premier Premium Class

Insurance Carrier: ______________________________

Insured: ______________________________

Policy Number: ______________________________

Policy Date: ______________________________

Date of Issue: ______________________________

Introduction

1. Clear explanation provides peace of mind.
2. First free service – referrals .... [ ]

Create Dollars for Future Delivery

1. Death Benefit $ ______________
2. Final Conversion date to convert to permanent insurance ______________
3. Policy will expire on______________________________

.... [ ]

The Contract

1. Incontestability – 2 years for your protection
2. Suicide – 1 year wait
3. Owner: ______________________________
4. Beneficiary: ______________________________
5. Grace period, 31 days for emergency use only
6. Use of dividends: This policy is not expected to contribute to divisible surplus and it is not expected that any dividends will be paid .... [ ]

Waiver of Premium

Waiver of premium – your peace of mind clause. After 6 months of total disability, Carrier will pay your premiums into the future. Refund. Carrier will also help you break into another job by paying your premiums for 2 years. Takes salary and vocation into consideration thereafter. Also allows conversion to Whole Life Paid Up at 90 even after disability begins.. [ ]

Continuity of Service

Introduce A Guide for the Future.. [ ]

Other Services Available.. [ ]

Policy Received by______________________________ Date ______________

Your Company / Name
and Contact Information

Appendix 5: One Page Business Plan Samples

Portland Insurance Agency

Consolidated Agency Plan

FY2008

vision

Within the next three years grow the Greater Portland Insurance Agency into a $15 million agency system with three locations providing auto, property & casualty, life insurance and financial services to individuals, families and businesses that are concerned about being protected from the unpleasant and unexpected events of life.

mission

Prepare and Protect the Families and Businesses in our community!

objectives

- Increase total revenue from $8 to $10 million in FY2008.
- Add 2,000 new policies in 2008 generating $1.2 million in incremental revenue.
- Increase average annual premium from $500 to $550.
- Increase client retention rate from 88.35% to 91%.
- Increase # of average appointments per agent from 1.9 to 5 per week by April 30th.
- Increase close rate from 25% to 50% by June 30th.
- Increase life insurance referrals from 2 to 5 per week per agent.
- Hire 5 new agents by April 1st, additional 7 new agents by October 1st.

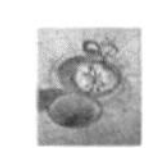

strategies

- Become locally known for excellence in "family & business insurance solutions".
- Build long term relationships w/ prominent bus. leaders - create consistent referral source.
- Maximize visibility by serving on community, non-profit, & professional boards.
- Mine existing client base for "A" clients; use seminar marketing system to find "B"clients.
- Strategic Mkting Alliances - align w/ CPA's, attorneys, auto dealers, real estate professionals.
- Sell thru education; use computer presentations to assure consistent message delivery.
- Staffing - hire professionals, provide quality training, 1:1 mentoring, reward Winners.
- Streamline all internal support & admin functions thru effective & smart use of technology.

action plans

- Implement agent incentive reward plan Jan. 15, 2008.
- Kickoff new agent search/hire process Feb. 1st; Training to begin April 15th.
- Contribute 1 article/month to Oregonian & Portland Tribune newspapers beginning Feb. 1st.
- Develop strat. relationship/Coop mktg program w/ major CPA firm & Law firm beg. 5/1.
- Conduct Credit Union member estate planning workshops every 8 weeks starting July 1st.
- Launch "Help a Non-Profit" initiative Sept. 30th.
- Re-launch High School Financial Program Oct. 1st.
- Move to new Portland Financial Center Nov. 1st.

www.onepagebusinessplan.com

Tri-Valley Financial Advisory Services

George Rask, CFP

FY2008

vision

By year-end 2010, grow George Rask, at Tri-Valley Advisory Services, into a $350,000 financial advisory service practice managing 40,000,000 in assets, providing trusted financial planning to 30 to 60 year-old clients for their retirement, and for their family's future wealth, who live in the greater Phoenix metro area.

mission

We help families provide for their families!

objectives

- Achieve 2008 production growth of 33%. Grow from $150,000 to $200,000.
- Boost return on assets from 0.20% to 0.40%.
- Increase assets from $21 million to $28 million.
- Maintain the same number accounts while culling lowest 10% of accounts from my BOB.
- Achieve asset-based revenue of 70% of BOB.
- Decrease transaction-based revenue from 38% to 30%.

strategies

- Focus on executing plan, frequent client contact, reviewing markets & client data.
- Capitalize on current clients, and planning and development of trends/opportunities.
- Attract new clients by consistently soliciting referrals in current BOB.
- Positive daily actions are focusing on contacts with clients, reduce administrivia.
- Increase face time with personalized mail campaigns, notes & flawless follow-up.
- Gather AUM by returning to my entire client list for additional assets each quarter.
- Grow assets by closing top 10 referral prospects I have on a monthly basis.

action plans

- Cull 10% of my accounts 2/15.
- Complete retraining on Financial Planning (CFP exam) by 3/15.
- Employ regular use of BIS beginning no later than 4/15.
- Utilize "Financial Planning System" for my top 10% clients beginning 6/15.
- Perform mid-year course correction, and revise business plan as necessary by 6/30.

 www.onepagebusinessplan.com

Tulsa Risk & Insurance Services

Susan McNalley

Four Month Plan

vision

In the next four months (Sept - Dec) grow my Tulsa PCS practice into a $12K/month revenue generating business specializing in personal P&C sales to high net worth individuals.

mission

Create peace of mind through proactive personal risk management.

objectives

- Achieve 2008 sales of $100,000.
- Work with prospects greater than or equal to $15K ICP 90% of the time.
- Call 35 prospects by Oct 31st.
- Implement suspect COI strategy w/ 114 suspect COIs in my database 9/1/08 to 1/1/09.
- Produce minimum of $12K in revenue every month in 2008; target $150,000.

strategies

- Leverage client and COI relationships for new business referrals to ICP prospects.
- Est. performance team via execution & accountability w/ AEs, Stews, MAA, & Claims.
- Develop suspect COIs w/Coninuous Contact COI Strategy Plan (CCCOISP)
- Grow business by asking for & working w/ICP clients.
- Ask every suspect COI for "test case or diagnostic" app w/ their clientele.
- Use direct mail for access to Top 50 prospects and large homes in target market.
- Confirm value and ask for referrals from clients at every meeting.
- Follow up w/ AE and Prospects on open cases weekly.
- Put all suspect COIs thru CCCOISP.

action plans

- Direct mail to large SGV homes by 9/30.
- Client-Confirm Value: ask 4 referrals 2 prospects/COIs.
- Mail letters and f-u by phone to Top 50 by Oct 15th.
- Mail /in-person (CCCOISP) 6 to 7 pre-determined items throughout year based on A,B, or C.
- Dial 114 suspect COIs by Nov 15th.

 www.onepagebusinessplan.com

Appendix 6: The Breakeven Budget Process

"The Marshmallow Experiment"

Little kids, ages 4-6, participated in a game of delayed gratification. It went like this:

A young child is seated at a table in an empty room. An experimenter enters and gives him a marshmallow saying, "If you can wait 15 minutes without eating this, I'll give you another one." About a third of the kids eat the marshmallow right away, another third squirm and writhe in desperation, while the remainder wait patiently for their reward.

See http://www.davidoverfield.com/210/the-marshmallow-test-delayed-gratification.

Which kid are you?

The kids who waited patiently – followed up three decades later – were more financially and personally successful than were those who couldn't wait.

Accounting systems can be seen in a similar light. Cash accounting – which only measures what goes in and what goes out monthly – doesn't look at the long term consequences of our behavior. We're always eating the "marshmallow" now.

For those who can wait, the accrual system is vastly superior. It allows you to set aside funds to meet future expenses.

How Cash Accounting Works

The cash accounting process (I want it now!) records the amount of income received and expenses paid each month. If income and expenses are in balance each month, and all bills are paid on time, then it gives the impression that your month-end checking account balance can be spent with no concern about future expenses. But, it works only if all your expenses are fixed and invariable. Is this ever true? Of course not. Many of your expenses vary from month to month. *A cash accounting system cannot tell you whether future income will cover future expenses.*

How Accrual Accounting Works

The accrual accounting process (I can wait!) works because it has a one-year, or longer, time horizon. For example, assume you have quarterly insurance premiums of $300. In January and February you have no payments due, but you have *accrued* $200 in future premiums due.

If you spend everything you make in January and February, you're going to be in trouble. You won't have enough money to pay the $300 insurance premium due in March. Multiply this event by your other deferred and variable expenses, and it is easy to see why a cash accounting method is a dangerous way to manage your money.

Accrual accounting records all expenses, for the entire year, and shows you how much money you need each month. Using our insurance example, accrual accounting requires that you set aside $100 each month. When the premium becomes due in the third month, you'll have set aside enough cash to pay the bill. By following this procedure for all your expenses such as taxes, cash reserves, future capital expenditures, retirement plan contributions and bonuses, you'll have peace of mind and enough cash to pay all your expenses.

It is human nature to spend everything we make. Setting aside funds for future expenditures – not eating the marshmallow – is a critically important factor in running a profitable business. The mere fact that you have cash in the bank at the end of the month is not an indication of profitability. The best way to know if you're profitable is to use accrual accounting. The Breakeven Budget™ makes it easy to use accrual accounting.

Available at SalesSolutionsPress.com.

Accrual Accounting or How to Use the Breakeven Budget™

We've provided 4 tools to make accrual accounting easy:

1 Chart of Accounts – Business Expenses

2 The Breakeven Business Budget

3 Chart of Accounts – Personal Expenses

4 The Breakeven Personal Budget

The first step in using the Breakeven Budget is to complete the Charts of Accounts.

The Charts of Accounts are divided into monthly and non-monthly categories. Each of the line items can be changed. You can insert or remove line items to meet your needs. The summary calculations are done automatically.

To complete the Charts of Accounts, you may need to review one, or perhaps two, years of past expenses. It is essential to record all expenses in order to generate a useful, accurate and helpful report.

In addition to past expenses, you must also enter your projected expenditures for long-term and future objectives, such as retirement planning, second home purchase, business capital expenditure projects, special marketing programs, and business expansion projects. Planning for future expenditures alone is enough reason to do comprehensive long-term planning. This type of planning is an important and often neglected part of many people's financial plans.

Steps to Complete the Business and Personal Charts of Accounts Forms

1 Review your previous year's expenses by listing every dollar you've spent on monthly and non-monthly expenses.

2 The items listed are guidelines for your use. Line inputs may be changed but the total number of lines cannot be changed.

3 All calculations are performed automatically. You only need to enter line item figures.

These business and personal worksheets will give you a one page summary of your current expenses. They will not tell you if you are profitable at this time because income is not listed.

You will have to complete the Chart of Accounts in order to complete the Breakeven Budget, but you will not have to complete the Chart of Accounts more than once – because a completed Breakeven Budget becomes the basis for each subsequent yearly budget.

Instructions for Completing the Breakeven Business / Personal Budget Forms

Completing the budget requires that you list all the line items on the Chart of Accounts worksheet. You must enter the line items in the month in which the expenses are actually due. When these entries are made, the software will calculate:

- Total annual expenses for each line item
  (e.g. total rent, total postage, etc.)
- Total monthly income
  (variable monthly income amounts are OK)
- Total monthly expenses
- +/- monthly cash flow
- +/- cumulative cash flow—This is the amount that should always be set aside in a deferred spending account to cover future expenses.

The Breakeven Budget Benefits

- Lists all expenses so that no expenses slip through a crack.
- Helps eliminate cash flow surprises.
- Provides a cash flow budget so that funds can be set aside in a deferred spending account to cover future expenses.
- Reveals profitability.

Creating the actual budget is very simple:

- Simply replace projected expenses with actual expenses as they are incurred. The software will automatically re-calculate your monthly totals.
- Add line items for any new expenses and enter costs (this, in effect, updates your Chart of Accounts).

Appendix 7: Practice Management Software

FAVORITE SMART PHONE

Blackberry Curve	www.blackberry.com	"Small, full keyboard, great calendar, contact and e-mail capability." – Laura S.
iPhone	www.apple.com	"I'm very impressed with its capabilities and Apple's customer service is awesome." – Elisa M.
Palm Treo	www.palm.com	"Easy to use and understand. It has an easy-to-see touch screen with large numbers and outstanding software to keep your appointments and contact information." – Gary R.
Blackberry Storm	www.blackberry.com	"It's easy to use and technology updates are easy to install." – Timothy H.
Motorola Q	www.motorola.com	"It works well with our office network."– Andrea G.

FAVORITE CELL PHONE SERVICE PROVIDER

Verizon	www.verizon.com	"I have used all the others and Verizon's coverage area and rate of dropped calls is superior to any other. Also, their customer service access and availability is second to none." – David B.
AT&T	www.att.com	"Impressive choice of plans. Great international coverage" – Sam K.
Sprint	www.sprint.com	"Sprint always works no matter where I am – even in the elevator." – Deborah H.
T-Mobile	www.t-mobile.com	"Best plan around for both work and home." – Stephanie L.
Alltel	www.alltel.com	"My phone service has excellent nationwide coverage." – Julia M.

*The information presented here was collected from a survey sent to all National Asscociation of Health Underwriters (NAHU) members in September 2009. Survey respondents supplied their own answers (the survey was not multiple choice). This column is not an NAHU endorsement of any of the companies or products listed here; it is simply a forum for NAHU members to share information about the companies they choose to work with.

Appendix 8: Daily Activity Report

Today's Date________________________________

I devoted__________ hours to making (setting) appointments for sometime in the near future.

_____a.m. to ____ a.m.

____ p.m. to ____p.m.

I had ____________ appointments.

_____a.m. to ____ a.m.

_____a.m. to ____ a.m.

____ p.m. to ____p.m.

____ p.m. to ____p.m.

I got____________ referrals today.

____

____

____

____

____

____

Paperwork is an activity best delegated to someone else! If you have to do it yourself, do it at the end of the day or very early in the beginning of the day.

Bibliography

A number of the following works are not cited in the text, but all contribute to my understanding of sales in the financial services industry.

Allen, David. *Getting Things Done*. New York: Penguin Books, 2003.

Bachrach, Bill. *Values-Based Selling*. San Diego: Aim High, 1996.

Beckwith, Harry. *Selling the Invisible*. New York: Warner Books, 1997.

Beckwith, Harry. *What Clients Love*. New York: Warner Books, 2003.

Bennett, Greg. *Consultative Closing*. New York: AMACOM, 2007.

Bossidy, Larry et.al. *Execution*. New York: Random House / Business Books, 2002.

Buckingham, Marcus and Curt Coffman. *First, Break All the Rules: What the World's Greatest Managers Do Differently*. New York: Simon and Schuster, 1999.

Buckingham, Marcus and Donald Clifton. *Now, Discover Your Strengths*. New York: Free Press, 2001.

Carson, Ron and Steven Sanduski. *Tested in the Trenches: A 9-Step Plan for Building and Sustaining a Million-Dollar Financial Services Practice*. Chicago: Dearborn Trade Publishing, 2005.

Cates, Bill CSP. CD tape series: *You Can Create a Referral Explosion:* Silver Springs, MD: Referral Coach International, 2001.

Clifton, Donald and Paula Nelson. *Soar with Your Strengths*. New York: Dell, 1995.

Collins, James. *Good to Great*. New York: HarperBusiness, 2001.

Covey, Steven. *7 Habits of Highly Effective People*. New York: Simon and Schuster, 1989.

Cerulli Associates. www.cerulli.com.

Daniels, David and Virginia Price. *The Essential Enneagram*. San Francisco: Harper, 2000.

Drucker, Peter F. *The Daily Drucker: 366 Days of Insight and Motivation for Getting the Right Things Done*. Oxford: Butterworth-Heinemann Ltd., 2004.

General Agents and Managers Association. http://www.gamaweb.com/index.htm.

Gerber, Michael E. *The E-Myth Revisited*. New York: HarperCollins, 2001.

Goldberg, Michael. *The 9 Ways of Working: How to Use the Enneagram to Discover Your Natural Strengths and Work More Effectively*. City: Marlowe & Company, 1999.

Green, Paul. *Get Hired!* Memphis: SkilFast, 2006.

Green, Paul. *Get Talent!* Memphis: SkilFast, Inc, 2007.

Grodzki, Lynn. *Building Your Ideal Private Practice*. New York: W.W. Norton, 2000.

Harrow, Susan. *Selling Yourself Without Selling Your Soul*. New York: Harper-Collins, 2002.

Horan, Jim. *The One Page Business Plan: Financial Services Edition*. Berkeley: The One Page Business Plan Company, 2008.

Jay, Mike, business coach and founder of B\COACH, a business coaching school.

Khalsa, Mahan et.al. *Let's Get Real or Let's Not Play*. City: Portfolio Hardcover, 2008.

Legolas, Charles, PhD. charles@criticalcontacts.com.

Macpherson, Duncan and David Miller. *Breakthrough Business Development*. New York: Wiley, 2007.

Maitri, Sandra. *The Spiritual Dimension of the Enneagram: Nine Faces of the Soul*. New York: Jeremy P. Tarcher, 2001.

Maselli, Frank. *Referrals: The Professional Way*. Franklin, MA: The Frank Maselli Company, 2005.

Miller, Robert B., Gary A. Williams and Alden M. Hayashi. *The 5 Paths to Persuasion: The Art of Selling Your Message.* New York: Warner Books, 2005.

Moeller, Steve. *Effort-Less Marketing for Financial Advisors.* Tustin, CA: American Business Visions, 1999.

Montoya, Peter. *The One Year Marketing Plan.* Tustin: Peter Montoya, Inc., 2007.

Montoya, Peter and Tim Vandehey. *The Brand Called You: The Ultimate Brand-Building and Business Development Handbook to Transform Anyone into an Indispensable Personal Brand.* New York: McGraw Hill, 2009.

Oberlin, Cliff and Jill Powers. *Building a High-End Financial Services Practice.* City: Bloomberg Press, 2004.

Rath, Tom. *Strengthsfinder 2.0.* City: Gallup Press, 2007.

Ray, Nick. "Green Light, Red Light, Yellow Light", www.coachnickray.com.

Stein, Dave. www.esresearch.com. Or call 1-508-313-9585.

Smith, Benson and Tony Rutigliano. *Discover Your Sales Strengths.* New York: Warner Books, 2003.

Tuleja, Tad et.al. *The New Strategic Selling.* New York: Warner Business Books, 2005.

Vessenes, Katherine and Peter. *Building Your Multi-Million Dollar Practice: 8 Success Strategies of Top Producing Advisors.* Chicago: Dearborn Trade Publishing, 2005.

Weisinger, Hendrie. *Emotional Intelligence at Work.* San Francisco: Jossey-Bass Publishers, 2000.

Willingham, Ron. *Integrity Selling for the 21st Century: How to Sell the Way People Want to Buy.* New York: Broadway Business, 2003.

Wright, Bruce. *The Wright Exit Strategy.* City: SAMMI Press, 1998.

Acknowledgements

First, I'd like to thank Ellen Reid, the Book Shepherd and her associates.

Jess Kennedy Williams – for transcribing my scribbled notes.

Blue Falcon Editing and Andrea Howe – for her initial editing.

Laren Bright – whose keen insight into my message helped with copy and title material.

Without Ellen and her team, this book wouldn't have been written.

Special thanks also go to Frank Maselli for his prospecting insights, Paul Green, Ph D. for his assistance about recruiting and interviewing, Howard D. Stevens of HR Chally for his assessments insights and advice, Barbara Spector of Smart Moves Inc. for her candidate assessment information, and Dave Stein of ES Research Group for his sales training advice. Jim Horan, president of the One Page Business Plan Company, provided valuable marketing and publishing advice. Charles Legolas, PhD, provided substantial foundational advice about natural target marketing. Without his keen insights, this book would have been significantly less useful.

Next, I'd like to thank Dyana Mardon, Terri Harel and Mia Pskowski, my able assistants who transcribed and interpreted my scribbled edits into readable texts.

I'd also like to thank Lisa Cornwell; without her keen editing this book would still be languishing in some computer file.

Finally, Lori Gudmundson and her husband David Milton have been the supporting force behind this book. Amazingly, they live on a boat thousands of miles away from my home in Berkeley, California, yet Skype and the internet keep us as close as next door neighbors. Lori's undying support has provided uninterrupted guidance and direction to this project. The look and feel of the book, and other details too numerous to mention, are the result of Lori's sense of design and editing.

Thank you.

The content of the book is ultimately mine.

Praise for Coach Nick Ray

Business Coaching at Its Best…

"Nick's coaching got me on target to achieve my business goals. His time management tools were very effective in ensuring I stayed focused on my goals in order to achieve the best results. He's great – he can do the same for you!"

Julianna Hynes, PhD
Leadership Development Consultant and Coach
Julianna Hynes & Associates

"Nick has a unique way of approaching the art of discovery. Under this method, you will work together and discover areas in your business that can be improved for positive results. His background and knowledge have been invaluable to me."

Bruce Johnson
Bruce Johnson Insurance Agency, LLC

"Nick helped me launch my solo practice after more than 20 years as an employee of other firms, assisting me in creating a business plan that leveraged my strengths, as well as dealing with the personal challenges of such a large transition in my career."

Michael Papanek

"Nick has the uncanny ability to quickly identify the areas I need to work on to improve my business. His tools and recommendations not only help me significantly increase my revenue, the satisfaction I get from the WAY I work now is tremendous. My career is custom tailored to take advantage of my particular strengths. I recommend his process to ALL of my advisor colleagues."

Kathy Troxell
Financial Advisor

"Nick's coaching has supported me with a more focused, consistent marketing plan that has resulted in a steady stream of new clients and new prospects."

Susan Danzig
Business Development Coach

"I have the highest respect and admiration for Nick. He is a person of utmost integrity and honesty, and if you are willing to follow his advice to the letter, you will be rewarded for your efforts."

Rande Shaffer
Shaffer Insurance & Risk Management

"Nick helped me get clarity with my business. He helped me to write a concise business plan that was to the point and then encouraged me to execute the plan. Thanks for all your help!"

Jerry Brunson
Exclusive Agent

"I have worked with Nick on two aspects of my business. One, increasing the amount of time off, and two, enhancing the productivity of my business. My time off has now increased so that I take off about eight weeks each year. Income has risen by more than 50%, so I have been able to enjoy both more leisure time and greater income. Having Nick as my coach gave me a fresh perspective and was the key to making this happen. My coach truly made a difference!"

Steven H. Way, CLU ChFC
Walnut Creek, CA

Interested or intrigued?

Here are your next steps:
Contact Nick for a COMPLIMENTARY coaching session
by email: nick@coachnickray.com or by telephone: 510.898.3245.
Check out Nick's website at www.coachnickray.com.

Also Available from Nick Ray

Nick offers these products as part of "A Financial Services Selling System for Top Producers."

Available Now!

10 Steps to Building a Referred Lead Engine Workbook

This workbook provides surefire ways to consistently obtain a continuous flow of high quality client referrals to your ideal prospects. Included in this workbook is a sample report about the Invisible Market Matrix and your Natural Target Market. This will make *10 Steps to Building a Referred Lead Engine* a supremely effective tool in your marketing efforts.

Building a Center of Influence Engine Workbook

Discover how to coordinate your Natural Target Market while developing relationships with Centers of Influence. This newly updated workbook reveals how to get high-quality referrals from those professionals serving your Target Market. *Building a Center of Influence Engine* provides a start-to-finish method for obtaining referrals from highly qualified professionals.

Available at SalesSolutionsPress.com.

New in 2010!

Target Marketing / Centers of Service Workbook

Discover how you can use the highest leverage and lowest effort marketing channel. This workbook shows you how to discover your Target Market, learn where your Target Market meets, and develop networks of vendors serving members of your Target Market. By using these methods, you have hit upon the best combination marketing program available!

Invisible Market Matrix Software

Do you know your Target Market chooses you? *The Invisible Market Matrix (IMM)* helps you discover the profile of your Target Market. The *IMM* is the bedrock tool for helping managers, recruiters and general agents improve agent selection. It also helps financial advisers improve their referred lead prospecting, whether the referrals come from clients, Centers of Influence, or Centers of Service. Using the *IMM* can transform your practice!

Do you want these practice builders as soon as they are available? Contact Nick at 510.898.3245 or at nick@coachnickray.com, and he'll let you know when they're hot off the press!